TOWARDS A RULES-BASED COMMUNITY: AN ASEAN LEGAL SERVICE

In 2007, ASEAN adopted the *ASEAN Charter,* which stated its ambition to become a 'rules-based' community respecting the rule of law. In order to fulfil this objective, it is vital that the necessary legal infrastructure has effective legal support. This book helps readers to understand the need for and role of such a legal service. To begin with, it explores the way ASEAN and its various institutions have evolved. The current situation with respect to the making of rules and settlement of disputes is then analysed, drawing not only on published primary and secondary materials, but also on the experience of diplomats, officials and legal officers. Finally, the authors draw on their practical experiences, as former attorney-general of an ASEAN member state and former head of the European Council legal service, to make recommendations on how an ASEAN Legal Service might be organised.

JEAN-CLAUDE PIRIS is President of Piris Consulting (European and Public International Law), a retired French Conseiller d'Etat, a former diplomat to the UN and former Director of Legal Affairs at the OECD, and was Director General of the Legal Service of the Council of the European Union for over 20 years. He has written several books with Cambridge University Press, most recently *The Future of Europe: Towards a Two-Speed EU?* (2012).

WALTER WOON is currently David Marshall Professor of Law at the National University of Singapore, the Dean of the Singapore Institute of Legal Education and President of the Goethe Institute Singapore.

He was formerly Attorney-General of Singapore, ambassador to the European Communities and several European countries, a member of the High Level Task Force to draft the ASEAN Charter and a nominated Member of Parliament. Professor Woon specialises in company law, criminal law and international law.

INTEGRATION THROUGH LAW

The Role of Law and the Rule of Law in ASEAN Integration

General Editors

J. H. H. Weiler, European University Institute
Tan Hsien-Li, National University of Singapore
Michael Ewing-Chow, National University of Singapore

The Association of Southeast Asian Nations (ASEAN), comprising the ten member states of Brunei Darussalam, Cambodia, Indonesia, Lao PDR, Malaysia, Myanmar, Philippines, Singapore, Thailand and Vietnam, has undertaken intensified integration into the ASEAN Community through the Rule of Law and Institutions in its 2007 Charter. This innovative book series evaluates the community-building processes of ASEAN to date and offers a conceptual and policy toolkit for broader Asian thinking and planning of different legal and institutional models of economic and political regional integration in the region. Participating scholars have been divided up into six separate thematic strands. The books combine a mix of Asian and Western scholars.

Centre for International Law, National University of Singapore (CIL-NUS)

The Centre for International Law (CIL) was established in 2009 at the National University of Singapore's Bukit Timah Campus in response to the growing need for international law expertise and capacity building in the Asia-Pacific region. CIL is a university-wide research centre that focuses on multidisciplinary research and works with other NUS or external centres of research and academic excellence. In particular, CIL collaborates very closely with the NUS Faculty of Law.

INTEGRATION THROUGH LAW
The Role of Law and the Rule of Law in ASEAN Integration
General Editors: J. H. H. Weiler, Tan Hsien-Li and Michael Ewing-Chow

TOWARDS A RULES-BASED COMMUNITY: AN ASEAN LEGAL SERVICE

JEAN-CLAUDE PIRIS
AND
WALTER WOON

CAMBRIDGE
UNIVERSITY PRESS

University Printing House, Cambridge CB2 8BS, United Kingdom

Cambridge University Press is part of the University of Cambridge.

It furthers the University's mission by disseminating knowledge in the pursuit of education, learning and research at the highest international levels of excellence.

www.cambridge.org
Information on this title: www.cambridge.org/9781107495265

© Centre for International Law 2015

This publication is in copyright. Subject to statutory exception and to the provisions of relevant collective licensing agreements, no reproduction of any part may take place without the written permission of Cambridge University Press.

First published 2015

A catalogue record for this publication is available from the British Library

Library of Congress Cataloging-in-Publication Data
Piris, Jean-Claude, author.
Towards a rules-based community: an ASEAN legal service / Jean-Claude Piris and Walter Woon.
    pages cm
Includes index.
ISBN 978-1-107-49526-5 (Paperback)
1. ASEAN. 2. Legal services–Southeast Asia. 3. Law–Southeast Asia–International unification. I. Woon, Walter C. M., author. II. Title.
KNE168.W66 2015
341.24′73–dc23   2014037661

ISBN 978-1-107-49526-5 Paperback

Cambridge University Press has no responsibility for the persistence or accuracy of URLs for external or third-party internet websites referred to in this publication, and does not guarantee that any content on such websites is, or will remain, accurate or appropriate.

CONTENTS

List of boxes *page* ix
Note on the authors x
General editors' preface xvii
Preface xxiii
List of abbreviations xxix

1. ASEAN as an organisation 1
   1.1 Chronology of the development of ASEAN 1
   1.2 ASEAN from its founding until the adoption of the ASEAN Charter 6
      1.2.1 A short history of ASEAN 6
      1.2.2 The institutional framework 16
   1.3 The ASEAN Charter and beyond 40
      1.3.1 The road to the Charter 40
      1.3.2 The ASEAN Charter and after 48

2. Towards an ASEAN community 65
   2.1 The current reality 66
      2.1.1 The making of rules 66
      2.1.2 The settlement of disputes 71
      2.1.3 Dispute settlement in practice 93
   2.2 Building the ASEAN Community 108
      2.2.1 The Community Blueprints 108
      2.2.2 Bali Concord III and the ASEAN Human Rights Declaration 111

3. The ASEAN Legal Service 113
   3.1 The European Union 113

CONTENTS

  3.1.1 The EU legal order 113
  3.1.2 The Legal Services of the Commission and of the Council of the EU 122
 3.2 Other international organisations 132
  3.2.1 Functions of a legal service in an international organisation 133
  3.2.2 Lessons drawn from the experiences of other international organisations 140
 3.3 Functions of an ASEAN Legal Service 145
  3.3.1 The necessity for a separate Legal Service 147
  3.3.2 Functions of the Legal Service 151
 3.4 Structure of an ASEAN Legal Service 167
  3.4.1 The choice of a single Legal Service 168
  3.4.2 Essential characteristics of the Legal Service 170
  3.4.3 Structure of the Legal Service 172
  3.4.4 Mission Statement and Terms of Reference 180
   Mission Statement 180
   Terms of Reference 180

Executive summary 183
Annex: major ASEAN agreements and declarations 191
Index 194

BOXES

Box 3.1 The infringement procedure   116

Box 3.2 The preliminary ruling procedure   119

NOTE ON THE AUTHORS

Jean-Claude Piris

President of Piris Consulting SPRL, a consulting firm on international issues, especially in European and public international law. Member of the Board of Trustees of the Academy of European Law, Trier, of the Advisory Board of the Centre for European Legal Studies, University of Cambridge, of the Scientific Board of the Robert Schuman Foundation, Paris and of the Governing Board of the European Institute for Public Administration, Maastricht. Member of the Audit Committee of the EU's Council.

Former Legal Counsel of the European Council (Heads of State or Prime Ministers of the EU member states) and of the EU Council of Ministers, Director General of the Legal Service of the Council (1988–2010). Jean-Claude Piris was the legal adviser of the intergovernmental conferences which negotiated and adopted the Treaties of Maastricht (1991–2), Amsterdam (1996–7), Nice (2000–1), the Constitutional Treaty (Rome, 2004) and Lisbon (2007). Barrister of the Council in a number of cases before the EU Court of Justice. Legal Director of the OECD (1985–8). French diplomat at the United Nations (1979–83). French Conseiller d'État (1972–2004). Senior Emile Noël Fellow at the Jean Monnet Centre of European Law and Fellow at the Straus Centre at NYU (2010–11). Alumnus École nationale d'administration

(ENA), postgraduate in Public Law (Paris), graduate in Political Science (Bordeaux).

Books

2013: *Il Trattato di Lisbona*; foreword by Giorgio Napolitano, President of the Italian Republic.

2012: *The Future of Europe: Towards a Two-Speed EU?* (Cambridge University Press); foreword by Joseph H. H. Weiler.

2010: *The Lisbon Treaty: A Legal and Political Analysis* (Cambridge University Press); foreword by Angela Merkel, Chancellor of the Federal Republic of Germany.

2007: *Il Processo di riforma dell'UE – Il trattato costituzionale nella prospettiva del trattato di riforma*; foreword by Giuliano Amato, Minister of Home Affairs, former Prime Minister of Italy.

2006: *The Constitution for Europe: A Legal Analysis* (Cambridge University Press).

2006: *Le traité constitutionnel pour l'Europe: une analyse juridique*; preface by Jean-Claude Juncker, Prime Minister of Luxembourg.

2006: *El tratado Constitucional para Europa: un análisis jurídico*; foreword by Alberto Navarro, Secretary of State of Spain for the EU.

Articles

Report of the Tommaso Padoa-Schioppa Group: 'Completing the Euro: A Road Map towards Fiscal Union in Europe' (Paris, 2012).

'Is It Time for the Euro Area to Develop Further Closer Cooperation among its Members?' (J. Monnet Papers, New York University, December 2011).

'Does the EU Have a Constitution? Does It Need One?' (Harvard Law School, 1999, *European Law Review*, also published in French, *RTDE*, and in German, *Europarecht*, 2000).

'The 1996 Intergovernmental Conference' (1995, *European Law Review*, also published in French, *RTDI*, 1995, in Spanish, *Gaceta Jurídica de la CEE*, 1995 and in Italian, *Il Diritto dell' Unione Europea*, 1996).

Lectures

King's College London, December 2013: 'The Five Crises in Europe and the Future of the EU' (E!Sharp on-line).

Ditchley (UK), 2012: 'A Two-Tier Europe and its Consequences'.

Brussels, European Parliament, 2012: 'Challenges of Multi-Tier Governance in the EU: Which Institutional Solutions?'

Berlin, Humboldt University, 2012: 'The Euro Crisis, Democratic Legitimacy and the Future Two Speed Europe'.

Oxford University, 2012: 'The Future of Europe: Towards a Two Speed EU?'

National University of Singapore, Centre for International Law, 2012: 'The Euro Crisis, Democratic Legitimacy and a Future Two Speed Europe'.

Ditchley, 2011: 'Who Holds the Power in Europe?'

Singapore, 2011: 'The EU Foreign Policy after the Lisbon Treaty'.

Harvard Law School, 2010: 'The EU External Relations'.

Conferences

At universities: Barcelona, Berlin (Humboldt), Brussels, Helsinki, Istanbul (Yeditepe), London, Cambridge, Oxford, Milan, Reykjavik, ENA (Strasbourg), Sciences-Po Paris, Collège d'Europe (Bruges), European University Institute (Florence), Fordham (New York), Columbia (New York), Harvard (Massachusetts), New York University, Victoria (British Columbia, Canada), National University of Singapore, University of International Business and Economics of Beijing.

To political authorities and senior officials: in Frankfurt (European Central Bank), Athens, Barcelona, Brussels, Bucharest, Copenhagen, Ditchley, Dublin, Helsinki, Linz, Madrid, Paris, Prague, Reykjavik, Rome, Vienna, Vilnius, Warsaw, etc. Three written submissions to the United Kingdom's House of Lords and House of Commons, at their request.

Decorations

Grand Officier de la Couronne (Belgique, 2013), Grand Cross in the Order of Knighthood of Henry the Navigator (Portugal, 2012), Commander in the Order of Orange-Nassau (Netherlands, 2011), Chevalier (1997) and Officier (2010) de la Légion d'Honneur (France), Grosse Goldene Ehrenzeichen mit dem Stern (Austria, 2002), Commander in the Order of Isabel la

NOTE ON THE AUTHORS

Católica (Spain, 1997), Ridder af 1 grad Dannebrogorden (Denmark, 1995).

Walter Woon

Professor Walter Woon read law at the National University of Singapore on a DBS Scholarship from 1977 to 1981. He graduated with an LLB (First Class Hons) in 1981 at the top of the class, winning the Adrian Clark Memorial Gold Medal. He was also awarded the Law Society of Singapore Book Prize (three times, in 1978, 1979 and 1980), the Leow Chia Heng Prize (1981) and the External Examiners' Special Cash Prize (1981). The same year he also topped the Postgraduate Practice Law Course (PLC), winning the Aw Boon Haw & Aw Boon Par Memorial Prize and the Tan Ah Tah Book Prize. He attended St John's College, Cambridge on a Commonwealth Scholarship from 1982 to 1983, graduating with an LLM (First Class Hons), and was awarded the Wright Prize and Whytehead Scholarship.

Professor Woon was called to the Singapore Bar in 1984 and was appointed Senior Counsel (equivalent of Queen's Counsel) in 2007. He has appeared in several cases before the Court of Appeal and in 1995 represented the Presidency in the only case to have come before the Constitutional Tribunal.

He was Sub-Dean and Vice-Dean of the Law Faculty of the National University of Singapore from 1988 to 1991. From 1992 to 1996 he was a Nominated Member of Parliament, during which time he introduced the Maintenance of Parents Act as a private member's bill, the only one to have been passed into law. He was Legal Adviser to the President and the Council of Presidential Advisers from 1995 to 1997.

NOTE ON THE AUTHORS

Between 1989 and 2001 he was a director of two companies listed on the Stock Exchange of Singapore, Intraco Ltd and Natsteel Ltd.

Between 1998 and 2006 Professor Woon was Singapore's Ambassador to Germany, Greece, the EU, Belgium, Luxembourg, the Netherlands and the Vatican. He was awarded the Grand Cross of the Order of St Gregory the Great in 2006.

Professor Woon was appointed second Solicitor-General in 2006, subsequently becoming Solicitor-General and then serving as Attorney-General of Singapore from 2008 to 2010. He also served as Judge Advocate General (2007–10), Member of the Board of Directors of the Monetary Authority of Singapore (2008–10) and Member of the Presidential Council for Minority Rights (2008–10).

In 2007 Professor Woon was an alternate member of the High Level Task Force to draft the ASEAN Charter. He functioned as delegation leader of the Singapore delegation in the latter half of the process and presented the completed Charter to the ASEAN leaders at the Thirteenth ASEAN Summit in Singapore (November 2007).

Professor Woon is currently David Marshall Professor at the Faculty of Law, National University of Singapore. He is concurrently Dean of the Singapore Institute of Legal Education, which oversees the Bar Examination and Foreign Practitioners Examination for persons seeking to practise law in Singapore. Professor Woon is also the Deputy Chairman of the Centre for International Law (CIL) National University of Singapore; the President of the Society for International Law Singapore (SILS); an Executive Committee

NOTE ON THE AUTHORS

Member of the Asian Society of International Law (Asian SIL); President of the Goethe Institute Society of Singapore; and an Honorary Fellow of the Singapore Institute of Directors (SID).

Professor Woon is the author of *Walter Woon on Company Law* (now in its 3rd edition), the standard text on Company Law in Singapore. His other publications include: *The Commercial Law of Singapore* (Cambridge, 1986); (with Andrew Hicks), *The Companies Act of Singapore – An Annotation* (1994, with supplements up to 2003); (as editor), *The Singapore Legal System* (1989); *Basic Business Law* (1994); (with Andrew Hicks), *The Companies Act of Malaysia – An Annotation* (1995, with supplements up to 2004); *The Annotated Statutes of Singapore*, vol. 1, *Companies and Securities Industry Acts* (1997); *Halsbury's Laws of Singapore*, vol. 6, *Company Law* (2000). His articles have also appeared in *Malayan Law Journal*, *Malaya Law Review*, *Securities Industry Review*, *Law Society Journal*, *Singapore Academy of Law Journal*, *Australian Journal of Corporate Law*, *Pacific Rim Law and Policy Journal* and *Korean Journal of International Law*. He is currently working on a Commentary on the ASEAN Charter for the Centre for International Law, National University of Singapore.

GENERAL EDITORS' PREFACE

This monograph is published within the context of a wide-ranging research project entitled, Integration Through Law: The Role of Law and the Rule of Law in ASEAN Integration (ITL), undertaken by the Centre for International Law at the National University of Singapore and directed by J. H. H. Weiler, Michael Ewing-Chow and Tan Hsien-Li.

The Preamble to the ASEAN Charter concludes with a single decision: "We, the Peoples of the Member States of the Association of Southeast Asian Nations ... [h]ereby decide to establish, through this Charter, the legal and institutional framework for ASEAN." For the first time in its history of over four decades, the Legal and the Institutional were brought to the forefront of ASEAN discourse.

The gravitas of the medium, a Charter: the substantive ambition of its content, the creation of three interlocking Communities, and the turn to law and institutions as instruments for realization provide ample justification for this wide-ranging project, to which this monograph is one contribution, examining ASEAN in a comparative context.

That same substantive and, indeed, political ambition means that any single study, illuminating as it may be, will cover but a fraction of the phenomena. Our modus operandi in this project was to create teams of researchers from Asia and elsewhere who would contribute individual monographs within an overall framework which we had designed. The project framework, involving several thematic clusters within each monograph, is thus determined by the framework and the place of each monograph within it.

As regards the specific content, however, the authors were free, indeed encouraged, to define their own understanding of the problem and their own methodology and reach their own conclusions. The thematic structure of the entire project may be found at the end of this Preface.

The project as a whole, and each monograph within it, display several methodological sensibilities.

First, law, in our view, can only be understood and evaluated when situated in its political and economic context. Thus, the first studies in the overall project design are intended to provide the political, economic, cultural and historical context against which one must understand ASEAN and are written by specialists in these respective disciplines. This context, to a greater or lesser degree, also informs the sensibility of each monograph. There are no "black letter law" studies to be found in this project and, indeed, even in the most technical of areas we encouraged our authors to make their writing accessible to readers of diverse disciplines.

Comparative experience suggests that the success of achieving some of the more ambitious objectives outlined in Article 1 of the Charter will depend in no small measure on the effectiveness of legal principles, legal rules and legal institutions. This is particularly true as regards the success of establishing "an ASEAN Community comprising the ASEAN Security Community, the ASEAN Economic Community and the ASEAN Socio-Cultural Community as provided for in the

GENERAL EDITORS' PREFACE

Bali Declaration of ASEAN Concord II". Article 2(2)(n) stipulates the commitment of ASEAN Member States to act in accordance with the principle of "adherence to multilateral trade rules and ASEAN's rules-based regimes for effective implementation of economic commitments and progressive reduction towards elimination of all barriers to regional economic integration." The ASEAN Member States therefore envisage that rules of law and the Rule of Law will become a major feature in the future of ASEAN.

Although, as seen, the Charter understands itself as providing an institutional and legal framework for ASEAN, the question of the "role of law and the rule of law" is not advocacy but a genuine enquiry in the various substantive areas of the project as to:

- the substantive legal principles and substantive rules of the various ASEAN communities;
- the procedural legal principles and rules governing institutional structures and decision-making processes;
- implementation, enforcement and dispute settlement.

One should not expect a mechanical application of this scheme in each study; rather, a sensibility that refuses to content itself with legal enactments as such and looks to a "living" notion of law and institutions is ubiquitous in all the studies. Likewise, the project is sensitive to "non Law." It variously attempts to locate the appropriate province of the law in this experience. That is, not only the role of law, but also the areas that are and should remain outside the reach of legal institutionalization with due sensitivity to ASEAN and Asian particularism and political and cultural identities.

GENERAL EDITORS' PREFACE

The project, and the monographs of which it is made, are not normatively thick. They do not advocate. They are designed, for the most part, to offer reflection, discuss the pros and cons, and in this way enrich public awareness, deepen understanding of different options and in that respect contribute indirectly to policymaking.

This decisive development of ASEAN has been accompanied by a growing Asian interest in various legal and institutional forms of transnational economic and political cooperation, notably the various voices discussing and showing an interest in an East Asia Integration project. The number of Free Trade Agreements (FTAs) and Regional Trade Agreements (RTAs) has increased from six in 1991 to 166 in 2013, with a further 62 in various stages of negotiations.

Methodologically, the project and many of the monographs are comparative in their orientation. Comparative law is one of the few real-life laboratories that we have in which to assess and understand the operation of different legal and institutional models designed to tackle similar objectives and problems. One should not need to put one's own hand in the fire to learn that it scorches. With that in mind a couple of monographs offer both conceptual reflection and pragmatic "tool boxing" on some of the key elements featuring in all regional integration systems.

Comparative law is in part about divergence: it is a potent tool and means to understand one's own uniqueness. One understands better the uniqueness of Apples by comparing them to Oranges. You understand better the specialness of a Toyota by comparing it to a Ford.

GENERAL EDITORS' PREFACE

Comparative law is also about convergence: it is a potent tool and means to understand how what are seemingly different phenomena are part of a broader trend, an insight which may enhance both self-understanding and policy potentialities.

Although many studies in the project could have almost immediate policy implications, as would the project as a whole, this is not its only or even principal purpose. There is a rich theory of federalism which covers many countries around the world. There is an equally rich theory of European integration, which has been associated with the advent Union. There is also considerable learning on Free Trade Areas and the like.

To date, the study of the legal aspects of ASEAN specifically and other forms of Asian legal integration has been derivative of, and dependent on, theoretical and conceptual insight which were developed in different contexts.

One principal objective of ITL and these monographs will be to put in place the building blocks for an authentic body of ASEAN and Asian integration theory developed in, and with sensitivity to, the particularities and peculiarities of the region and continent. A theory and conceptual framework of Asian legal integration will signal the coming of age of research of and in the region itself.

Although the monographs form part of an overarching project, we asked our authors to write each as a "standalone" – not assuming that their readers would have consulted any of the other titles. Indeed, the project is rich and few will read all monographs. We encourage readers to pick and choose from the various monographs and design their own menu.

GENERAL EDITORS' PREFACE

There is, on occasion, some overlap in providing, for example, background information on ASEAN in different studies. That is not only inevitable but desirable in a project of this amplitude.

The world is increasingly witnessing a phenomenon of interlocking regional organization where the experience of one feeds on the others. In some way, the intellectual, disciplinary and comparative sensibility of this project is a microcosm of the world it describes.

The range of topics covered in this series comprises:

The General Architecture and Aspirations of ASEAN
The Governance and Management of ASEAN: Instruments, Institutions, Monitoring, Compliance and Dispute Resolution
Legal Regimes in ASEAN
The ASEAN Economic Community
ASEAN and the World
The Substantive Law of ASEAN

PREFACE

ASEAN is an organisation propelled by a mixture of idealism and hot air. From its inception as a confidence-building association in 1967 to the ambitious adoption in the 2011 Bali Concord III of an ASEAN common platform on global issues, there have been many idealistic statements and declarations. The great failing of ASEAN, repeatedly identified by successive Secretaries-General and the Eminent Persons' Group on the ASEAN Charter, has been the failure to follow up on the grand designs with concrete measures.

Idealism was the primary driver of the ASEAN Charter, which came into force in December 2008. Hitherto, ASEAN had functioned without a formal legal structure. There was in fact no treaty governing the structure and administration of the organisation. Business was done on an ad hoc basis. It was felt that after four decades some formal legal structure had to be given to the organisation if it was to be fit to meet the challenges of the twenty-first century.

The level of ambition is high. The declared goal is to create by 2015 an ASEAN Community comprising three pillars: the ASEAN Economic Community (AEC), the ASEAN Political-Security Community (APSC) and the ASEAN Socio-Cultural Community (ASCC). None of this will work unless there is an infrastructure of law. Indeed, in the ASEAN Charter and subsequent declarations by the leaders of the ASEAN member states, the rule of law is repeatedly emphasised, as is the desire to make ASEAN a rules-based organisation. Good governance and human rights are also underlined. All of this requires a firm legal basis, which ASEAN has hitherto lacked.

There is a dearth of material on the legal history of ASEAN and the ASEAN Charter. In order to understand the necessity for a proper legal service, it is essential to appreciate how ASEAN came into being and what its present shape is. This monograph is not meant to be a theoretical exposition of what a perfect ASEAN should be, much less is it a comparative study of other regional and international organisations. In writing this monograph, the authors have drawn on their own personal experiences rather than scholarly material written by academics. The theory is one thing; reality is quite another. Secondary literature (with few exceptions) comes from people who are not participants but merely observers from afar; for this reason there has been little citation of academic writings. When drafting the Charter, the High Level Task Force did not refer to academic sources at all. Much of what is contained in the first two chapters is a distillation of the source material (viz. the numerous ASEAN declarations, road maps, plans of action and other documents) in the light of the authors' experience and discussions with the actual participants.[1]

---

[1] Much of the material in these chapters is the result of research done by one of the authors for a Commentary on the ASEAN Charter. This material will appear again in the Commentary when it is published.

PREFACE

Nor is this monograph aimed primarily at the academic community. Rather, the audience is the practitioners: the diplomats, politicians and officials that make ASEAN run. The object of the authors is to provide an overview of how ASEAN came to be what it is, what the organisation is like now and why the creation of a proper legal service is crucial to its development into a rules-based law-abiding ASEAN Community.

The first chapter of this monograph sketches the history of ASEAN. Without this basic understanding of the history of the organisation it is impossible to understand the deeply held aversion to formal structures and procedures. ASEAN's origin as an association of non-Communist countries in Southeast Asia seeking to build trust among themselves in a dangerous world is described for the convenience of those unfamiliar with this history (which unfortunately includes most citizens of ASEAN member states, who often are taught more in school about the history of Europe than that of Southeast Asia). It is important to understand the origins of ASEAN in order to appreciate why the 'ASEAN way' is what it is. The first part of Chapter 1 also traces the development of the various organs of ASEAN – the ASEAN Summit, the ASEAN Ministerial Meeting, the ASEAN Economic Ministers' Meeting, the Secretary-General, the ASEAN Secretariat and the multifarious ministerial meetings that have been established over the years. Much of the practice in ASEAN is not documented. It is necessary to plough through the many ASEAN documents and put them in some order so that this background can be appreciated. Without knowledge of how ASEAN has evolved over the last four and

PREFACE

a half decades there is no context for the legal service. This brief overview will, it is hoped, give the reader some idea of that evolution. An understanding of the alphabet soup of acronyms representing the various subgroups and organs of ASEAN is essential to a proper appreciation of the future development of the ASEAN Community.

The second half of Chapter 1 describes and analyses the evolution of the ASEAN Charter, which now forms the legal foundation of the ASEAN Community. The Charter is not quite a constitution, but it provides the legal basis for the development of the ASEAN Community. It is not the object of this monograph to explain every facet of the Charter. Rather, four significant aspects are dealt with in particular: dispute settlement, the Community Councils, the Secretary-General and Secretariat and the Committee of Permanent Representatives. These were innovations designed to ensure the proper working of the ASEAN Economic Community (AEC), the ASEAN Political-Security Community (APSC) and the ASEAN Socio-Cultural Community (ASCC). These provide the basis for the future evolution of ASEAN from an association into a rules-based, people-centred community.

Chapter 2 examines how the theory (as set out in the numerous declarations, road maps, plans of action, etc. issued after ASEAN meetings) squares with practice, focusing in particular on how rules are made and disputes settled. An organisation which aims to be rules-based needs to have a coherent method for making those rules. The first part of the chapter describes how the process has hitherto been carried out, which can only be described as extremely ad hoc. Crucially, the rule of law requires a proper means to settle disputes in a legally binding manner. The next part of the chapter therefore describes and analyses in detail the theoretical framework of agreements governing dispute settlement. The chapter goes on to examine how this actually works in reality, focusing on the few cases involving ASEAN member states that have reached the stage of international adjudication. The aim is to provide the reader with a better appreciation of what 'the ASEAN way' means in practice. The chapter concludes with a survey of the blueprints for the establishment of the ASEAN Economic Community (AEC), the ASEAN Political-Security Community (APSC) and the ASEAN Socio-Cultural Community (ASCC).

Chapter 3 makes the case for the establishment of a proper ASEAN Legal Service. The first part of the chapter describes the experience of other intergovernmental and supranational organisations. However, it must be appreciated that ASEAN has no ambition to become a supranational entity; there is no political desire for an ever-closer union. During the drafting of the Charter it was clearly understood that the EU is not a model for ASEAN. Nonetheless, the legal services of the EU are described in order to provide a backdrop against which to consider the role of such a legal service in the development of ASEAN as a rules-based, law-abiding organisation. The object of the exercise is to provide some pointers on how the proposed ASEAN Legal Service might be structured. It is always wise to learn from others and adapt rather than attempt to rebuild from scratch what others have done before.

The role of an ASEAN Legal Service would include: drafting rules and regulations, providing the institutional legal

PREFACE

memory of ASEAN, giving legal advice, assisting in monitoring the implementation of and compliance with ASEAN instruments, representing the organisation in legal proceedings and providing support for the dispute settlement process. The second part of the chapter is devoted to setting out the possible structure of such a legal service, drawing on the authors' respective experiences as heads of the legal service of an ASEAN member state and the EU.

The object of this monograph is to provoke thought about the legal underpinnings of the ASEAN Community. This is absolutely essential if ASEAN is to achieve its ambitions. It is easy to proclaim that ASEAN shall become a rules-based community in which the rule of law, human rights and good governance are basic principles. Achieving that aim is the difficult part. Sceptics might dismiss all of this as mere hot air. But, as the Montgolfier brothers demonstrated, hot air, properly harnessed, can lift a man to the heavens.

ABBREVIATIONS

AANZFTA	ASEAN–Australia–New Zealand Free Trade Area
ACB	ASEAN Compliance Body
ACC	ASEAN Coordinating Council
ACIA	ASEAN Comprehensive Investment Agreement
ACMB	ASEAN Compliance Monitoring Body
ACT	ASEAN Consultation to Solve Trade and Investment Issues
ADMM	ASEAN Defence Ministers' Meeting
AEC	ASEAN Economic Community
AECC	ASEAN Economic Community Council
AEM	ASEAN Economic Ministers' Meeting
AFMM	ASEAN Finance Ministers' Meeting
AFTA	ASEAN Free Trade Area
AHMM	ASEAN Health Ministers' Meeting
AHRD	ASEAN Human Rights Declaration
AIA	ASEAN Investment Area
AICHR	ASEAN Intergovernmental Commission on Human Rights
AIELN	Asian International Economic Law Network
AIPO	ASEAN Inter-Parliamentary Organisation
ALAWMM	ASEAN Law Ministers' Meeting
ALMM	ASEAN Labour Ministers' Meeting

ABBREVIATIONS

AMAF	Meeting of the ASEAN Ministers of Agriculture and Forestry
AMCA	Meeting of ASEAN Ministers Responsible for Culture and the Arts
AMEM	ASEAN Ministers on Energy Meeting
AMM	ASEAN Ministerial Meeting (meeting of the Foreign Ministers)
AMME	ASEAN Ministerial Meeting on the Environment
AMMin	ASEAN Ministerial Meeting on Minerals
AMMST	ASEAN Ministerial Meeting on Science and Technology
AMMTC	ASEAN Ministerial Meeting on Transnational Crime
AMRDPE	ASEAN Ministers on Rural Development and Poverty Eradication
AMRI	ASEAN Ministers Responsible for Information
APSC	ASEAN Political-Security Community
ASC	ASEAN Standing Committee (consisting of foreign ministry officials)
ASCC	ASEAN Socio-Cultural Community
ASEAN-ISIS	ASEAN Institutes of Strategic and International Studies
ASEC	ASEAN Secretariat
ASED	ASEAN Education Ministers' Meeting
ASLOM	ASEAN Senior Law Officials' Meeting
ASOD	ASEAN Senior Officials on Drug Matters
ATIGA	ASEAN Trade in Goods Agreement
ATM	ASEAN Transport Ministers' Meeting
CCI	Coordinating Committee on Investment
CEPT	Common Effective Preferential Tariff

ABBREVIATIONS

CLMV	Cambodia, Laos, Myanmar and Viet Nam
COREPER	Comité des représentants permanents/Committee of Permanent Representatives
CPR	Committee of Permanent Representatives
DG	Directorate-General
DLAPIL	Directorate of Legal Advice and Public International Law
DSG	Deputy Secretary-General
DSM	dispute settlement mechanism
EPG	Eminent Persons' Group
EU	European Union
FMM	Finance Ministers' Meeting
HLTF	High Level Task Force
HPA	Hanoi Plan of Action
ICJ	International Court of Justice
JMM	Joint Ministerial Meeting
M-ATM	ASEAN Tourism Ministers' Meeting
PMC	Post-Ministerial Conference
PR	Permanent Representative
QMV	qualified majority voting
SEANWFZ	Treaty on the Southeast Asia Nuclear Weapon-Free Zone (1995)
SEOM	Senior Economic Officials' Meeting
SOM	Senior Officials' Meeting (comprising foreign ministry officials)
TAC	Treaty of Amity and Cooperation in Southeast Asia (1976)
TELMIN	ASEAN Telecommunications and IT Ministers' Meeting
TEU	Treaty on European Union

ABBREVIATIONS

TFEU	Treaty on the Functioning of the European Union
UNSC	United Nations Security Council
VAP	Vientiane Action Programme
WTO	World Trade Organization
ZOPFAN	Zone of Peace, Freedom and Neutrality Declaration (1971)

Chapter 1

ASEAN as an organisation

1.1 Chronology of the development of ASEAN

1967 Signing of the ASEAN Declaration in Bangkok on 8 August by the Foreign Ministers of Indonesia, Malaysia, the Philippines, Singapore and Thailand, marking the foundation of the association. This counts as the first ASEAN Ministerial Meeting (AMM). The AMM meets annually thereafter. Creation of the ASEAN Standing Committee (ASC) to prepare meetings of the AMM.

1971 ASEAN Senior Officials' Meeting (ASEAN SOM) established to discuss sensitive issues before submission to the ASEAN Ministerial Meeting (AMM). The SOM leader is the permanent secretary or equivalent.

1973 Foreign Ministers decide to establish an ASEAN Secretariat.

1975 End of the Vietnam War with the fall of South Vietnam. ASEAN Economic Ministers meet for the first time in Bali (the next meeting in Kuala Lumpur the following year adopted the name ASEAN Economic Ministers' Meeting). ASEAN Labour Ministers (ALMM) meet in Jakarta and thereafter biannually.

1976 First ASEAN Summit held in Bali. Issue of the Declaration of ASEAN Concord (Bali Concord).

ASEAN AS AN ORGANISATION

Signing of the Treaty of Amity and Cooperation in Southeast Asia (TAC). Establishment of the ASEAN Secretariat in Jakarta.

1977 Second ASEAN Summit held in Kuala Lumpur. ASEAN Economic Ministers' Meeting (AEM) formalised. Establishment of the Senior Economic Officials' Meeting (SEOM). The AEM meets annually thereafter. ASEAN Education Ministers (ASED) meet for the first time in Manila; meetings are held irregularly thereafter.

1978 Invasion of Cambodia by Vietnamese forces. Special meeting of ASEAN Foreign Ministers held in January 1979 to deplore the invasion. ASEAN diplomats thereafter work together to deny diplomatic recognition to the new regime in Cambodia.

1980 Establishment of the ASEAN Ministers of Health Meeting (AHMM), ASEAN Ministerial Meeting on Science and Technology (AMMST) and ASEAN Ministers on Energy Meeting (AMEM).

1981 ASEAN Ministerial Meeting on the Environment (AMME) held in Manila for the first time.

1986 ASEAN Law Ministers' Meeting (ALAWMM) established, to be held every thirty-six months thereafter with Senior Law Officials' Meetings (ASLOMs) in between.

1987 Brunei joins ASEAN. Third ASEAN Summit held in Manila.

1989 Conference of Ministers Responsible for Information (AMRI) inaugurated.

1991 Withdrawal of Vietnamese forces from Cambodia and election of a new government.

1.1 CHRONOLOGY OF THE DEVELOPMENT OF ASEAN

1992 Secretary-General of the ASEAN Secretariat redesignated as Secretary-General of ASEAN and given an enhanced role carrying with it ministerial status. ASEAN Secretariat ostensibly professionalised by open recruitment of staff rather than nomination by member states.

1992 Fourth ASEAN Summit held in Singapore. Signing of the Agreement on Common Effective Preferential Tariff Scheme for the ASEAN Free Trade Area (AFTA) and the Framework Agreement on Enhancing ASEAN Economic Cooperation.

1995 Vietnam joins ASEAN. Fifth ASEAN Summit held in Bangkok. Signing of the Treaty on the Southeast Asia Nuclear-Weapon-Free Zone (SEANWFZ). ASEAN Transport Ministers' Meeting (ATM) held for the first time and annually thereafter.

1996 First informal ASEAN Summit held in Jakarta, marking the de facto inauguration of annual meetings of the heads of state/government.

1997 Laos and Myanmar join ASEAN. Cambodia's application to join is postponed because of a coup in the country. Second Informal ASEAN Summit held in Kuala Lumpur, marking the thirtieth anniversary of the founding of ASEAN. ASEAN Vision 2020 adopted. ASEAN Finance Ministers' Meeting (AFMM) and ASEAN Ministerial Meeting on Transnational Crime (AMMTC) established. Asian financial crisis impacts ASEAN member states severely.

1998 Sixth ASEAN Summit held in Hanoi, the first to be hosted by one of the new member states. Hanoi Action

Plan launched to realise the Vision 2020. Conclusion of the Framework Agreement on the ASEAN Investment Area (AIA). Establishment of the ASEAN Tourism Ministers' Meeting (M-ATM). First meeting of the ASEAN Ministers on Rural Development and Poverty Eradication (AMRDPE).

1999 Cambodia joins ASEAN. This rounds off the current membership of the organisation. Inauguration of the ASEAN Foreign Ministers Retreat, allowing the Foreign Ministers to discuss issues informally.

2001 From this year ASEAN Summits are held annually. ASEAN Telecommunications and IT Ministers' Meeting (TELMIN) established.

2002 Framework Agreement on Comprehensive Economic Cooperation between ASEAN and China. This is the first of several such agreements with external partners. Subsequently, agreements have been entered into with Japan, India, South Korea, Australia and New Zealand.

2003 Ninth ASEAN Summit held in Bali. Adoption of the Declaration of ASEAN Concord II (Bali Concord II). Leaders declare their intention to establish an ASEAN Community consisting of three pillars: political and security cooperation, economic cooperation and socio-cultural cooperation. Meeting of ASEAN Ministers Responsible for Culture and the Arts (AMCA) established.

2004 Tenth ASEAN Summit held in Vientiane; Protocol on Enhanced Dispute Settlement Mechanism adopted by the Economic Ministers. Vientiane Action Programme (designed to deepen economic integration and narrow

1.1 CHRONOLOGY OF THE DEVELOPMENT OF ASEAN

the development gap) replaces the Hanoi Plan of Action. ASEAN Socio-Cultural Community Plan of Action and the ASEAN Security Community Plan of Action adopted, with a commitment to work towards the development of an ASEAN Charter. Legal unit in the ASEAN Secretariat set up. ASEAN Consultation to Solve Trade and Investment Issues (ACT) and the ASEAN Compliance Body (ACB) established.

2005 Eleventh ASEAN Summit held in Kuala Lumpur. ASEAN heads of state/government issue the Declaration on the Establishment of the ASEAN Charter. Eminent Persons' Group (EPG) formed. ASEAN Ministerial Meeting on Minerals (AMMin) established.

2006 ASEAN Defence Ministers' Meeting (ADMM) established.

2007 Twelfth ASEAN Summit held in Cebu in January 2007. Cebu Declaration on the Blueprint for the ASEAN Charter issued endorsing the Report of the Eminent Persons' Group and setting up a High Level Task Force (HLTF) for Drafting of the ASEAN Charter. HLTF completes work on the Charter. Completed Charter presented to the Heads of State/Government at the Twelfth ASEAN Summit in Singapore on 20 November 2007. ASEAN Economic Community Blueprint adopted.

2008 Creation of the ASEAN Political-Security Community Council (APSC), the ASEAN Economic Community Council (AECC) and the Socio-Cultural Community Council (ASCC). ASEAN Coordinating Council

(ACC) and Committee of Permanent Representatives (CPR) established. ASEAN Charter comes into force on 15 December 2008.

2009 Declaration on the Roadmap for the ASEAN Community (2009–15) adopted at the Fourteenth ASEAN Summit in Cha-Am, Thailand. Initiative for ASEAN Integration Workplan 2 replaces the Vientiane Action Programme. ASEAN Intergovernmental Commission on Human Rights (AICHR) established in October 2009 at the Fifteenth ASEAN Summit in Cha-Am, Thailand.

2010 Protocol to the ASEAN Charter on Dispute Settlement Mechanisms (the DSM Protocol) signed by the Foreign Ministers at the Sixteenth ASEAN Summit in Hanoi.

2011 Declaration on 'ASEAN Community in a Global Community of Nations' (Bali Concord III) issued at the Nineteenth ASEAN Summit in Bali.

2012 ASEAN Human Rights Declaration (AHRD) adopted by the ASEAN leaders at the Twenty-first ASEAN Summit in Phnom Penh, Cambodia.

1.2 ASEAN from its founding until the adoption of the ASEAN Charter

1.2.1 *A short history of ASEAN*

The Association of Southeast Asian Nations was founded on 8 August 1967 by means of the Bangkok Declaration (officially, the ASEAN Declaration), a modest document that did

1.2 ASEAN FROM ITS FOUNDING

not even purport to be a treaty.[1] The Bangkok Declaration did not create an organisation. What it sought to do was to set up a mechanism to foster mutual trust among the original five founder states.

At the time of ASEAN's founding Southeast Asia was in an unsettled state. Malaysia was formed in 1963, comprising the Federation of Malaya and the former British colonies in Southeast Asia, namely Singapore, British North Borneo (Sabah) and Sarawak.[2] Indonesia had opposed this, seeing it as a neocolonialist plot and an impediment to unification of the Malay archipelago.[3] The idea of an Indonesia Raya (Greater Indonesia) had germinated during the Japanese occupation of 1942–5. Indeed, Indonesia's success in incorporating Dutch

---

[1] The Bangkok Declaration was signed in Bangkok by the Foreign Ministers of Indonesia (Mr Adam Malik), Malaysia (Tun Abdul Razak, who was Deputy Prime Minister rather than Foreign Minister), the Philippines (Mr Narciso Ramos), Singapore (Mr S. Rajaratnam) and Thailand (Mr Thanat Khoman). The Heads of State/Government were not involved.

[2] Brunei declined to join Malaysia and remained under British protection until 1984, becoming a member of ASEAN that same year. See Declaration of the Admission of Brunei Darussalam into ASEAN, signed in Jakarta on 7 January 1984.

[3] The history of the Malay independence movement and its Pan-Indonesian ambitions is recounted in Cheah Boon Kheng, *Red Star Over Malaya*, 3rd edn (Singapore University Press, Singapore, 2003), chap. 4. The suspicions of the independence generation of Indonesians regarding the British are understandable, given the part that British and Indian troops played in restoring Dutch rule in the East Indies after the Japanese surrender in September 1945.

New Guinea in 1963[4] may have given fresh life to the ambition to realise an Indonesia Raya. The Philippines too opposed the formation of Malaysia because of its claim to Sabah.[5] Indonesian hostility to Malaysia led to an undeclared war (euphemistically termed Konfrontasi, from the Dutch word for 'confrontation'). Though fighting took place primarily along the jungle border between East Malaysia and Indonesian Kalimantan, there were repeated attempts to infiltrate Peninsular Malaysia (including a paratroops drop in the southern state of Johore) and one notorious incident where Indonesian marines detonated a bomb at MacDonald House in Singapore, killing three civilians. Konfrontasi came to an end with the fall of President Soekarno in October 1965 after an abortive Communist coup.

However, all was not well even within Malaysia. Tensions between the state government of Singapore and the federal government in Kuala Lumpur came to a head in 1965 over the incendiary issue of whether the new Malaysian federation would be multiracial (a line espoused by the People's Action Party in Singapore) or communal (which was the leitmotiv of Malayan politics ever since the demise of the short-lived Malayan Union in 1948). These tensions led to the ejection of Singapore from the Malaysian federation in

---

[4] After the success of the Indonesian revolution, the only portion of the Dutch East Indies to remain under the suzerainty of the Netherlands was Western New Guinea. This was placed under United Nations administration in 1962 and transferred to Indonesia in 1963. See Britannica Online (www.britannica.com) under 'Papua: History'.

[5] See Rodolfo Severino, *Southeast Asia in Search of an ASEAN Community* (ISEAS Publishing, Singapore, 2006), pp. 2, 164–6.

1.2 ASEAN FROM ITS FOUNDING

August 1965.[6] On the northern border of Peninsular Malaysia, the remnants of the Communist Malayan People's Liberation Army lurked in the jungles of Thailand, continuing to pose a sporadic danger even after the end of the Malayan Emergency.[7] Relations between Singapore and Indonesia were fraught after the conviction for murder in 1966 of the Indonesian marines who had perpetrated the MacDonald House bombing.[8] Continued tensions between Malaysia and the Philippines over Sabah had led to the postponement of the Fourth ASEAN Ministerial Meeting, which was supposed to have been held in 1970 in Manila.[9]

Looming over all these disputes was the shadow of the Vietnam War. The unspoken motive for the formation of ASEAN was fear of Communist expansion. It was felt that cooperation among the five non-Communist states of Southeast Asia was essential to meet the challenge. Four of the five founders were aligned to the Western bloc. As US allies, the Philippines and Thailand played host to American bases.

---

[6] The story is told (albeit from only one side) in Lee Kuan Yew, *The Singapore Story: Memoirs of Lee Kuan Yew* (Times Editions, Singapore, 1998).

[7] This was a Communist insurrection lasting from 1948 until 1960, when it was officially declared to be over. See Richard Clutterbuck, *The Long, Long War: The Emergency in Malaya 1948–1960* (Cassell, London, 1966).

[8] The Indonesian marines were in civilian clothes. They were tried and convicted of murder, the Federal Court in Singapore holding that they had forfeited the right to be treated as prisoners of war: see *Osman v. Public Prosecutor* [1965–67] SLR (R) 402. The decision of the Federal Court was affirmed by the Privy Council [1968–70] SLR (R) 117.

[9] The Fourth AMM finally took place in March 1971.

ASEAN AS AN ORGANISATION

Singapore was home to the major British naval base in the Far East, while the Training Depot for the British Brigade of Ghurkhas was in Sungei Patani in West Malaysia. Indonesia was non-aligned and determined to remain so. ASEAN was not conceived as a military or security organisation. Given the unhappy history of international relations amongst the five original member countries, the primary objective of ASEAN was the fostering of trust amongst the member states in order to meet the Communist threat and keep Southeast Asia free of big power rivalries.[10]

The foundation of ASEAN did not lead to an immediate outburst of fraternal feeling. In an assertion of newly independent Singapore's prickly sovereignty, the Indonesian marines who had perpetrated the MacDonald House bombing were hanged in October 1968, an act which provoked severe anti-Singapore riots in Indonesia.[11] Also in 1968, information surfaced about a Filipino plot to infiltrate saboteurs in Sabah.[12] Meanwhile, North Vietnam had launched the Tet offensive in 1968, which demonstrated to the world that the war would not be won by America. Racial riots racked Malaysia in May 1969, threatening to spill over into

---

[10] See the Preamble to the 1967 ASEAN Declaration. The first four paragraphs emphasise the need for regional cooperation, solidarity and partnership while the final two paragraphs make plain the desire to exclude external meddling in the politics of the member states.

[11] Lee, *From Third World to First*, pp. 37–8.

[12] Severino, *Southeast Asia*, p. 164. See also http://countrystudies.us/philippines/93.htm. This website contains online versions of books previously published by the Federal Research Division of the Library of Congress.

1.2 ASEAN FROM ITS FOUNDING

Singapore.[13] It was against this backdrop that in 1971 ASEAN issued the ZOPFAN Declaration,[14] which was 'inspired by the worthy aims and objectives of the United Nations, in particular by the principles of respect for the sovereignty and territorial integrity of all states, abstention from threat or use of force, peaceful settlement of international disputes, equal rights and self-determination and non-interference in affairs of States', according to its Preamble.

North Vietnam's victory over South Vietnam in 1975 gave a new impetus to regional cooperation. The heads of state/government[15] of ASEAN met for the first time in Bali in February 1976. Two major results of the First ASEAN Summit were the Declaration of ASEAN Concord (or the Bali Concord, as it is known) and the Treaty of Amity and Cooperation (commonly referred to as the TAC).[16] The Bali

---

[13] Lee, *From Third World to First*, pp. 38–40.
[14] Officially, the Zone of Peace, Freedom and Neutrality Declaration, signed in Kuala Lumpur on 27 November 1971 by the Foreign Ministers of Indonesia (Mr Adam Malik), Malaysia (Tun Abdul Razak, who was by then Prime Minister and Foreign Minister), the Philippines (Mr Carlos Romulo), Singapore (Mr S. Rajaratnam) and Thailand (Mr Thanat Khoman, then Special Envoy of the National Executive Council). For the background to this, see Severino, *Southeast Asia*, pp. 166–7.
[15] ASEAN Summits are meetings of the heads of government. Ceremonial heads of state (e.g., the King of Thailand, the President of Singapore and the Yang di-Pertuan Agong of Malaysia) do not attend.
[16] The Bali Concord and the Treaty of Amity and Cooperation were both signed on 24 February 1976 in Denpasar, Bali by the President of Indonesia (Mr Soeharto), the Prime Minister of Malaysia (Dr Hussein Onn), the President of the Philippines (Mr Ferdinand Marcos), the Prime Minister of Singapore (Mr Lee Kuan Yew) and the Prime Minister of Thailand (Mr Kukrit Pramoj). Brunei ratified the Treaty of Amity and

Concord solemnly declared that 'Member states, in the spirit of ASEAN solidarity, shall rely exclusively on peaceful processes in the settlement of intra-regional differences'. The member states renounced the use of force and committed themselves to settlement of differences or disputes by peaceful means in Article 2 of the TAC.

The end of the Vietnam War posed a challenge to ASEAN. The fall of South Vietnam, followed shortly by Communist takeovers in Cambodia and Laos, created a fear that Thailand would be next. However, despite the gloomy prognostications of doomsayers at the time, it was Cambodia and not Thailand that provided the stage for the next act of the drama. In December 1978 Vietnamese forces invaded Cambodia and overthrew the Khmer Rouge regime. This placed the members of ASEAN in a quandary: Pol Pot and the Khmer Rouge were odious, but it would be an unfortunate precedent to acquiesce to a regime change imposed by Vietnamese bayonets. The ASEAN Foreign Ministers held a special meeting to 'deplore' the Vietnamese invasion.[17] The fear was of an escalation of fighting and an incursion across the Thai border.[18] The situation in Indochina would occupy the political attention of ASEAN for more than a decade.

The diplomatic struggle over recognition of the new Cambodian government was a defining experience for

Cooperation in Southeast Asia (TAC) on 6 June 1987. Accession to the TAC has become a prerequisite for membership of ASEAN.

[17] See the Joint Statement issued after the Special Foreign Ministers' Meeting (Bangkok, January 1979).

[18] See the Joint Communiqué of the Twelfth AMM (Bali, June 1979).

1.2 ASEAN FROM ITS FOUNDING

ASEAN. ASEAN diplomats worked together in the United Nations and other international forums to ensure that the use of force to change a government was not legitimised. This cooperation forged close relationships among the members of that generation of diplomats who were on the front line of the campaign to deny recognition of the Vietnamese-installed Cambodian government.[19]

After more than a decade, the Cambodian imbroglio ended in 1991 with the withdrawal of Vietnamese forces and the election of a new government in Cambodia. At that point, it was felt that the inclusion of the Indochinese countries was necessary to ensure that there would be no recurrence of hostilities. Rapprochement came quickly. Vietnam joined ASEAN in 1995,[20] followed by Laos in 1997.[21] At the same time, Myanmar also joined the organisation despite the chorus of international criticism following the military crackdown on civilian protesters after the general election.[22]

---

[19] Former Singapore Foreign Minister Wong Kan Seng at the S. Rajaratnam Lecture, 23 November 2011.

[20] Declaration of the Admission of the Socialist Republic of Viet Nam into the Association of Southeast Asian Nations, signed in Bandar Seri Begawan, Brunei Darussalam, on 28 July 1995. Vietnam had acceded to the Treaty of Amity and Cooperation in Southeast Asia (TAC) on 22 July 1995, having ratified it on 30 May.

[21] Declaration on the Admission of the Lao People's Democratic Republic into the Association of Southeast Asian Nations, signed in Subang Jaya, Malaysia, on 23 July 1997. Laos had acceded to the Treaty of Amity and Cooperation in Southeast Asia (TAC) on 29 June 1992 and ratified it on 17 July 1996.

[22] Declaration on the Admission of the Union of Myanmar into the Association of Southeast Asian Nations, signed in Subang Jaya,

ASEAN AS AN ORGANISATION

Cambodia's accession was delayed due to a coup by Second Prime Minister Hun Sen against First Prime Minister Prince Norodom Ranariddh.[23] The process of rounding out the membership of ASEAN was finally completed with the accession of Cambodia in 1999.[24]

The accession of the four new members (commonly referred to by the acronym CLMV) demonstrated the inclusiveness of the ASEAN ideal. There were no preconditions as to form of government or political system. There was no shared history or culture binding the new members to the old, no common language or religion. The governing philosophy was entirely pragmatic. These were countries within Southeast Asia and had to be brought within the family group, warts and all.

It is easy in the light of this history to understand the aversion to outside interference in the internal affairs of member states. Suspicion of former colonial masters and big

---

Malaysia, on 23 July 1997. Myanmar ratified the Treaty of Amity and Cooperation in Southeast Asia (TAC) on 10 July 1996, having acceded to it on 27 July 1995.

[23] See Britannica Online (www.britannica.com) under 'Cambodia: Cambodia since 1990'. The Joint Statement of the Special Meeting of the ASEAN Foreign Ministers on Cambodia (Kuala Lumpur, July 1997) glosses over this completely. Cambodia had made a formal application to join ASEAN, which was accepted at the Twenty-ninth AMM (Jakarta, July 1996).

[24] Declaration on the Admission of the Kingdom of Cambodia into the Association of Southeast Asian Nations, signed in Hanoi, Vietnam on 30 April 1999. Cambodia ratified the Treaty of Amity and Cooperation in Southeast Asia (TAC) on 25 July 1995, having acceded on 25 January 1995.

1.2 ASEAN FROM ITS FOUNDING

powers runs deep. Even within the family suspicions remain. There is a fairly high degree of trust and comfort among the founding members and Brunei (commonly referred to as ASEAN-6), born of the baptism by fire of the Vietnamese invasion of Cambodia. This narrative of ASEAN solidarity is not shared by the newer members. At the S. Rajaratnam Lecture 2011[25] Singapore's former Foreign Minister Wong Kan Seng recounted how ASEAN diplomats had worked closely together for over a decade to deny international recognition of the Cambodian government installed by the Vietnamese after the invasion in 1978. At the end of the lecture the Cambodian ambassador stood up to make the point that the Vietnamese had not invaded Cambodia but had instead liberated the Cambodian people from the horrors of the Pol Pot regime. This lack of a shared narrative is a fault line that separates the CLMV countries from the ASEAN-6. In many ways they still remain outsiders. The process of building trust still remains a challenge.[26] Shared sovereignty in the EU style was never on the agenda. For the young states of Southeast Asia, any erosion of their hard-won sovereignty is not

---

[25] Held at the Shangri-La Hotel, Singapore, 23 November 2011.

[26] As illustrated by the very public disagreement between Cambodia on one hand and the Philippines and Vietnam on the other over the latter's disputes with China in the South China Sea. This led to an unprecedented failure to issue a joint communiqué at the conclusion of the Forty-fifth AMM held in Phnom Penh in July 2012. Cambodia came under intense criticism and felt it necessary to issue a press statement on 26 July 2012 defending its chairmanship. The lack of fraternal feeling was again in evidence at the subsequent Twenty-first ASEAN Summit in Phnom Penh, where the Cambodian chair again came in for criticism over the way it handled the South China Sea issue.

ASEAN AS AN ORGANISATION

something that can or will be easily accepted. This should be borne firmly in mind when considering the stop–go evolution of ASEAN into a community.

1.2.2 The institutional framework

There has been no strategic grand plan mapping out the development of the institutional framework of ASEAN. Indeed, ASEAN functioned without such a framework for many years after its foundation. The institutions developed pragmatically, impelled by need rather than vision. This section describes how the various ASEAN bodies came into being.

(1.2.2.1) The ASEAN Ministerial Meeting and the ASEAN Summit

The founders of ASEAN did not set out to create an international organisation with a separate personality. Indeed, the ASEAN Declaration merely provided for an annual meeting of Foreign Ministers, known as the ASEAN Ministerial Meeting (AMM).[27] To support the work of the Foreign Ministers, a standing committee (the ASEAN Standing Committee or ASC) was also created, under the chairmanship of the country hosting the AMM. Initially, this comprised the ambassadors to the host of the next AMM. In 1992 this was changed to directors-general in charge of ASEAN at the respective foreign ministries, together with the Secretary-General.[28] In

---

[27] The very first AMM was the one at which the ASEAN Declaration was adopted on 8 August 1967.
[28] Severino, *Southeast Asia*, p. 22.

1.2 ASEAN FROM ITS FOUNDING

1971 senior officials from the ministries of foreign affairs began meeting regularly at the ASEAN Senior Officials' Meeting (ASEAN SOM), a body which was not specifically created by any agreement but which evolved naturally. SOM was established to discuss political issues, especially sensitive ones, before submission to the AMM. The SOM leader was generally the permanent secretary (or his equivalent in countries that did not adopt the British nomenclature) of the ministry. From the start ASEAN was driven by the foreign ministries of the member states, the other ministries being kept on the sidelines for the most part. The AMM is the most durable of the ASEAN institutions and continues to play a significant role in the steering of the organisation. It has met annually since 1967.[29] After the First ASEAN Summit (Bali, February 1976) it was clarified that the AMM was the principal organ for the coordination of overall policy direction for ASEAN.[30] The ASC was charged with conduct of ASEAN external relations.

In addition to the formal meetings, the Foreign Ministers held special meetings when necessary.[31] The AMM

---

[29] Except for 1970, when the Philippines was host. The meeting was postponed owing to disagreements between the Philippines and Malaysia over Sabah. The AMM met again only in March 1971.

[30] This was proclaimed in the Joint Communiqué of the Ninth AMM (Manila, June 1976). Although it was stated that this role was in accordance with the Declaration of ASEAN Concord (Bali Concord), there is actually nothing said explicitly in that document.

[31] For instance, in 1997 to discuss the situation in Cambodia. It was decided to postpone Cambodia's accession to ASEAN because of the fighting between political factions in the country.

evolved into an occasion for engaging the dialogue partners[32] as well, in the Post-Ministerial Conferences (PMCs). In 1999 the ASEAN Foreign Ministers Retreat was inaugurated, to enable frank and open discussion of issues of common interest in an informal setting away from the formal proceedings of the AMM. Initially, the retreats were held in conjunction with the AMM but from 2001 separate retreats were hosted by member states other than the AMM host. From its rather modest beginnings the AMM evolved into one of the main motors of ASEAN. The Foreign Ministers' agenda grew steadily over the years, judging by the length and substance of the communiqués issued after each AMM.

The main policy-making body of ASEAN was the ASEAN Summit, a meeting of the heads of state[33] and government of the member states. It was not originally envisaged in the Bangkok Declaration that the heads of state and government would meet. Indeed, the first Summit was held in Bali only in February 1976, nearly nine years after the Bangkok Declaration. In the interim, the Vietnam War had come to an end with the precipitate withdrawal of the USA and the collapse of the non-Communist governments of Vietnam, Cambodia and Laos. The sound of falling dominoes was in the air.

---

[32] At the time of writing the dialogue partners are: Australia, Canada, China, the European Union, India, Japan, New Zealand, the Republic of Korea, the Russian Federation and the USA.

[33] The Summit is confined to executive heads of state. Ceremonial heads of state like the Yang di-Pertuan Agong of Malaysia, the President of Singapore and the King of Thailand do not attend.

1.2 ASEAN FROM ITS FOUNDING

One of the main results of the First ASEAN Summit was the Declaration of ASEAN Concord ('Bali Concord'), which provided for meetings of heads of government 'as and when necessary'. The need for greater cooperation in the political, economic, social and cultural fields was emphasised. Security cooperation was to be on a non-ASEAN basis between member states 'in accordance with their mutual needs and interests'. All the members of ASEAN agreed to sign the Treaty of Amity and Cooperation in Southeast Asia (TAC),[34] which committed the parties to the peaceful settlement of disputes. The UN General Assembly at its 47th Session in 1992 endorsed the TAC, recognising that it provides a strong foundation for regional confidence-building and cooperation.[35] The member states also committed themselves to improving the ASEAN machinery, inter alia by studying the desirability of a new constitutional framework. This desire was only fulfilled three decades later when the ASEAN Charter was adopted.

A second Summit was held in Kuala Lumpur the following year, at which the AEM was formalised. After that there was a ten-year hiatus until the Third ASEAN Summit in Manila in 1987, held against the backdrop of the continuing Vietnamese occupation of Cambodia. The major diplomatic result was the amendment of the TAC to allow for the

---

[34] Accession to the TAC has become an essential step in membership of ASEAN. Since then eighteen other countries and the European Union have also become parties.

[35] A/Res/47/53B adopted by consensus on 9 December 1992.

accession of states outside Southeast Asia.[36] The Summit Declaration stated that ASEAN would 'continue and intensify efforts to find a durable comprehensive solution to the Kampuchean problem'.

Summit meetings continued to be held at irregular intervals, the fourth taking place in Singapore in January 1992. The Fourth Summit was the first one after the settlement of the Cambodian problem and marked a shift in focus to economic matters. Two major economic agreements were signed: the Agreement on the Common Effective Preferential Tariff (CEPT) Scheme for the ASEAN Free Trade Area and the Framework Agreement on Enhancing ASEAN Economic Cooperation. In the Singapore Declaration issued on 28 January 1992 the leaders declared the intention that ASEAN move to a higher plane of political and economic cooperation. It was announced that an ASEAN Free Trade Area (AFTA)

---

[36] At the time of writing the following have acceded to the TAC (see the Table of Ratifications maintained by the ASEAN Secretariat on its website: www.asean.org): Papua New Guinea (10 August 1989); the People's Republic of China (8 October 2003); India (8 October 2003); Japan (2 July 2004); Pakistan (2 July 2004); Republic of Korea (27 November 2004); the Russian Federation (29 November 2004); Australia (28 July 2005); Mongolia (28 July 2005); New Zealand (28 July 2005); France (13 January 2007); Timor Leste (13 January 2007); Bangladesh (1 August 2007); Sri Lanka (1 August 2007); the European Communities and European Union (28 May 2009); Democratic People's Republic of Korea (24 July 2008); the United States of America (22 July 2009); Canada (23 July 2010); Turkey (23 July 2010); Brazil (17 November 2012). The United Kingdom, Norway and Serbia have also expressed interest in acceding to the TAC: see the Chairman's Statements of the Twentieth and Twenty-first ASEAN Summits (Phnom Penh, April 2012 and November 2012 respectively).

1.2 ASEAN FROM ITS FOUNDING

would be established using the CEPT Scheme, the deadline for reduction of tariffs being 2007.[37] Formal Summit meetings would be held every three years, with informal Summits in the intervening period. A ministerial council was to 'supervise, implement and review' the CEPT Scheme.[38] The Senior Economic Officials' Meeting (SEOM) was tasked to handle all aspects of ASEAN economic cooperation.

The Fifth Summit was held in Bangkok in December 1995. Vietnam had just become a member of ASEAN and the vision of bringing all Southeast Asian countries within the fold was progressing nicely.[39] The Treaty on the Southeast Asia Nuclear Weapon-Free Zone (SEANWFZ) was signed. This established a commission consisting of the Foreign Ministers of the parties, which was to meet as and when necessary on the request of a state party, preferably in conjunction with the AMM.[40] The Fifth Summit was followed by the first and second informal ASEAN Summits, which were held in Jakarta (30 November 1996) and Kuala Lumpur (14–16 December

---

[37] The deadline was moved forward twice: see Severino, *Southeast Asia*, p. 225. By 2003, AFTA in the ASEAN-6 (viz., the original members plus Brunei) had been realised. The CLMV countries had until 2010 to do so: see the Report of the Eminent Persons' Group on the ASEAN Charter, para. 14 n. 5.

[38] This council was to consist of one nominee from each member state chosen by the AEM, together with the Secretary-General: Agreement on the CEPT Scheme for the ASEAN Free Trade Area, Article 7. The AFTA Council's membership overlapped with that of the AEM but was not identical.

[39] Laos and Cambodia attended as observers. They joined ASEAN in 1997 and 1999 respectively.

[40] Treaty on the Southeast Asia Nuclear Weapon-Free Zone, Article 8.

1997).[41] The 1997 Summit was declared to be a commemorative Summit, marking the thirtieth anniversary of the founding of ASEAN. ASEAN Vision 2020 was adopted by the leaders as a programme to bring ASEAN into the twenty-first century.

The Sixth ASEAN Summit took place in Hanoi in December 1998, followed by two more informal Summits in Manila (27-28 November 1999) and Singapore (22-25 November 2000). Thereafter, the pace of summitry picked up, with annual Summits from 2001 until the Thirteenth Summit in 2007.[42]

The Ninth ASEAN Summit in Bali (October 2003) saw the adoption of the Declaration of ASEAN Concord II (Bali Concord II). It was a significant gesture, referring back to the original Bali Concord issued at the First ASEAN Summit twenty-seven years previously. Bali Concord II was a re-imagining of the ASEAN idea. In it the leaders of the member states declared their intention to establish an ASEAN Community consisting of three pillars: political and security cooperation, economic cooperation and socio-cultural cooperation. The first pillar was the longest-established,

---

[41] In order to coordinate between the AMM and AEM, a Joint Ministerial Meeting (JMM) had been created at the Third Summit (Manila, 1987). However, continued rivalry between the AMM and AEM made it difficult in practice to convene the JMM. It was decided that the solution lay in holding more frequent meetings of the leaders, which led to the convening of the informal annual Summits in the gap between the official ones.

[42] There were actually two Summits in 2007: in Cebu, the Philippines, 9-15 January and in Singapore, 18-22 November 2007. The Cebu Summit was postponed from December 2006 on account of a typhoon threat.

1.2 ASEAN FROM ITS FOUNDING

political dialogue having been driven by the Foreign Ministers since the foundation of ASEAN. The second pillar, economic cooperation, had been progressing in parallel with the first ever since the First ASEAN Summit in 1976. The third pillar was new, sweeping together other activities that did not belong under the first two pillars. The Joint Ministerial Meeting (JMM) was revived, comprising the AMM, AEM, AFMM and the Secretary-General.[43] Bali Concord II paved the way for the eventual adoption of the ASEAN Charter at the Thirteenth Summit in Singapore in November 2007.

By the first decade of the twenty-first century, the ASEAN Summit had become the major event in the life of the organisation. ASEAN had broadened out its reach to engage dialogue partners like Japan, China, the Republic of Korea (which collectively came to be known as ASEAN+3), India, Australia, the EU and the USA. Meetings with external partners were held back-to-back with the Summits. Framework agreements for closer economic cooperation were concluded with major dialogue partners.[44] The logic of economic

---

[43] This had been established at the Third Summit (Manila, 1987).

[44] Such an agreement had already been concluded with China in 2002: see the Framework Agreement on Comprehensive Economic Cooperation between ASEAN and China. At the Ninth Summit in 2003 agreements were signed with India and Japan: see the Framework Agreement on Comprehensive Economic Cooperation between India and ASEAN and the Framework Agreement for Comprehensive Economic Partnership between Japan and ASEAN. The Eleventh Summit in Kuala Lumpur saw the conclusion of the Framework Agreement on Comprehensive Economic Cooperation among the Governments of Member Countries of ASEAN and the Republic of Korea (2005).

integration led to a spate of ASEAN economic agreements.[45] The pace and intensity of the meetings made it necessary to double the number of Summits per year, which was done when the ASEAN Charter came into force in December 2008.

(1.2.2.2) The ASEAN Economic Ministers' Meeting and SEOM

For much of the first two decades of ASEAN's life the focus had been on economic cooperation as opposed to integration. ASEAN Economic Ministers had first met in November 1975 at the behest of Indonesia.[46] At the First ASEAN Summit in Bali the following year the leaders agreed that the Economic Ministers would meet 'to consider measures to be taken to implement the decisions of the [ASEAN Summit] on matters of economic cooperation'.[47] This was formalised in the Bali Concord signed at that Summit.[48] The ASEAN Economic Ministers' Meeting (AEM)[49] took place annually, preceded by a Senior Economic Officials' Meeting (SEOM). The AEM and SEOM did not report to the Foreign Ministers

---

[45] ASEAN Framework Agreement for Integration of Priority Sectors (Vientiane, November 2004); Protocol on Enhanced Dispute Settlement Mechanism (Vientiane, November 2004); Agreement to Establish and Implement the ASEAN Single Window (Kuala Lumpur, December 2005); Agreement on the Harmonized ASEAN Electrical and Electronic Equipment Regulatory Regime (Kuala Lumpur, December 2005).

[46] Severino, *Southeast Asia*, p. 214.

[47] Joint Communiqué of the First ASEAN Summit, para. 9.

[48] Declaration of ASEAN Concord (Bali Concord), para. 5.

[49] This nomenclature was adopted at the second Economic Ministers' Meeting in Kuala Lumpur (March 1976). It was institutionalised by the Second ASEAN Summit the next year.

1.2 ASEAN FROM ITS FOUNDING

but rather progressed on their own path independently.[50] For better coordination, a JMM of Foreign and Economic Ministers was established by the Third ASEAN Summit in 1987.[51] The Fourth ASEAN Summit in Singapore in 1992 gave a push for greater economic integration of ASEAN. SEOM was tasked with handling all aspects of ASEAN economic cooperation. Oversight would be provided by the Economic Ministers. This economic pillar took a life of its own separate from the diplomatic track that hitherto had dominated ASEAN. From the founding of ASEAN in 1967, it was the foreign ministries who had been in the driver's seat steering the organisation. The creation of an ASEAN Free Trade Area necessitated a much closer involvement of the various economic ministries in ASEAN affairs.

Over the years the AEM and SEOM acquired a whole host of supervisory and monitoring functions in order to realise the vision of creating an integrated economic area. These functions were conferred by various agreements

---

[50] Though the Foreign Ministers took the opportunity in their AMM joint communiqués to 'commend' or express appreciation for the work of their economic colleagues in fostering ASEAN economic cooperation. The AMM also 'noted' agreements entered into by the Economic Ministers.

[51] The Joint Communiqué of the Twenty-third AMM (Jakarta, July 1990) announced the convening of the inaugural ASEAN Joint Ministerial Meeting of Foreign and Economic Ministers. In practice, it proved difficult to convene the JMM regularly owing to the competition between the Foreign and Economic Ministers. The JMM was expanded to include the Finance Ministers and the Secretary-General by the Ninth ASEAN Summit (Bali, October 1993): see the Joint Communiqué of the Thirty-seventh AMM (Jakarta, June 2004).

entered into by the ASEAN member states. The first two were the Agreement on the CEPT Scheme for the ASEAN Free Trade Area and the Framework Agreement on Enhancing ASEAN Economic Cooperation, both signed in 1992 at the Fourth Summit in Singapore. The AEM was tasked with reviewing the progress of implementation of the latter agreement.[52] At the Fifth ASEAN Summit in 1995 a Framework Agreement on Services was signed, the aim of which was to liberalise trade in services beyond the commitments undertaken under the General Agreement on Trade in Services (GATS) and to substantially eliminate restrictions to trade in services.[53] SEOM was charged with facilitation, supervision and review of the agreement.[54] In 1998 SEOM was tasked with monitoring the implementation of the ASEAN Framework Agreement on Mutual Recognition Arrangements, reporting to the AFTA Council.[55] That same year saw the conclusion of the Framework Agreement on the ASEAN Investment Area. The AEM was to create an AIA Council comprising ministers in charge of investment.[56] The AIA Council in turn established a Coordinating Committee on Investment (CCI) consisting of senior officials from ministries and government

---

[52] 1992 Framework Agreement on Enhancing ASEAN Economic Cooperation, Article 8.
[53] 1995 ASEAN Framework Agreement on Services, Article I.
[54] Ibid., Article XI.
[55] ASEAN Framework Agreement on Mutual Recognition Arrangements, Article 13.
[56] Framework Agreement on the ASEAN Investment Area, Article 16. The membership of the AIA Council overlaps with that of the AEM but is not identical.

1.2 ASEAN FROM ITS FOUNDING

agencies responsible for investment. The CCI reported to the AIA Council through SEOM.[57] A further monitoring role for SEOM was given in the e-ASEAN Framework Agreement 2000, with reports going to the AEM.[58] In 2004 a Framework Agreement for Integration of Priority Sectors was signed in Vientiane; again, SEOM was tasked with assisting the Economic Ministers with oversight, monitoring and coordination.[59] SEOM was also given a key role in the settlement of economic disputes by the Protocol on Enhanced Dispute Settlement Mechanism.[60]

The High Level Task Force on ASEAN Economic Integration recommended the reaffirmation of the AEM's role as coordinator for all ASEAN economic integration and cooperation issues. Technical issues were to be resolved by SEOM, while issues of a policy nature were to be resolved by the AEM, AFTA Council and AIA Council. These recommendations were adopted in Bali Concord II.[61]

The AEM took place back-to-back with meetings of the AFTA Council and later the AIA Council which was set up under the Framework Agreement on the ASEAN

---

[57] Ibid., Article 16(5).
[58] E-ASEAN Framework Agreement, Article 13. This was signed at the Fourth Informal Summit (Singapore, November 2000).
[59] 2004 ASEAN Framework Agreement for Integration of Priority Sectors, Article 19.
[60] Signed by the Economic Ministers at the Tenth ASEAN Summit in Vientiane, 29 November 2004.
[61] See para. 14 of the HLTF's recommendations, which were annexed to the Declaration of ASEAN Concord II, signed by the leaders in Bali at the Ninth ASEAN Summit on 7 October 2003.

Investment Area.[62] Both these Councils were overseen by the AEM. The first decade of the new millennium also saw increasing economic engagement with dialogue partners outside ASEAN. The ultimate aim was to create a free trade area between ASEAN and the respective partners. Framework agreements for the creation of closer economic ties were entered into with China, Japan, India and the Republic of Korea.[63] The AEM played a coordinating role in negotiations for deepening economic cooperation under these framework agreements, supported by SEOM.[64]

Thus, on the eve of the adoption of the ASEAN Charter the AEM was the major organ steering the economic integration of ASEAN. The AEM came to play a role of equal importance to the AMM in the creation of the ASEAN community.

---

[62] Framework Agreement on the ASEAN Investment Area (1998), Article 16.

[63] For the sake of completeness, it should be mentioned that an Agreement Establishing the ASEAN–Australia–New Zealand Free Trade Area was concluded in 2009, after the entry into force of the ASEAN Charter.

[64] See, e.g., the Framework Agreement on Comprehensive Economic Cooperation between India and ASEAN and China, Article 12; Framework Agreement on Comprehensive Economic Cooperation between India and ASEAN (2004), Article 12; Framework Agreement on Comprehensive Economic Cooperation among the Governments of Member Countries of ASEAN and the Republic of Korea (2005), Article 5.3; Agreement Establishing the ASEAN–Australia–New Zealand Free Trade Area (2009), Chapter 16, Article 1(6). A Framework Agreement for Comprehensive Economic Partnership between Japan and ASEAN was also signed in 2003. Untypically, no specific mention was made of the role of the AEM. Nonetheless, the ASEAN–Japan Committee on Comprehensive Economic Partnership reported to the AEM.

1.2 ASEAN FROM ITS FOUNDING

(1.2.2.3) The Secretary-General and ASEAN Secretariat

At the Sixth AMM in Pattaya, Thailand (April 1973) the Foreign Ministers decided that the time had come to establish a central Secretariat for ASEAN. Indonesia volunteered to play host.[65] There was a competing offer from the Philippines to site the Secretariat in Manila, but after negotiation this was withdrawn 'in the interest of regional unity and harmony'.[66] However, it was only in 1976 that the member states finally established the ASEAN Secretariat (ASEC) by means of an agreement signed by the Foreign Ministers.[67] An Agreement relating to privileges and immunities of the ASEAN Secretariat was executed by Indonesia on 20 January 1979, giving juridical personality to ASEC under Indonesian law and granting diplomatic privileges to the Secretary-General and officers of ASEC.[68]

The Secretary-General of the ASEAN Secretariat was appointed on a rotational basis for a two-year term.[69] The first Secretary-General was Mr Hartono Rekso Dharsono of Indonesia,[70] a former general and diplomat. In

---

[65] Joint Communiqué of the Sixth AMM, para. 8.
[66] Joint Communiqué of the Seventh AMM (Jakarta, May 1974), para. 8.
[67] Agreement on Establishment of the ASEAN Secretariat, signed in Bali on 24 February 1976.
[68] The Agreement was signed by the Secretary-General on behalf of ASEAN.
[69] Ibid., Article 3.
[70] His appointment was confirmed at the Ninth AMM (Manila, June 1976). He was replaced in 1978 by Mr Umarjadi Njotowijono, who served out the remainder of his term. Mr Umarjadi was followed by Ali bin Abdullah (Malaysia), Narciso Reyes (Philippines), Chan Kai Yau (Singapore) and Phan Wanannamethe (Thailand).

1985 the term of office of the Secretary-General was extended to three years.[71] The Secretary-General's function was to take charge of ASEC. He was personally to attend all meetings of the AMM as secretary.[72] He was also to attend meetings of the ASC and other ASEAN committees or similar bodies in order to keep himself informed of their activities. Where necessary, he was to explain the directives of the ASC to the other committees or bodies. In short, the Secretary-General was meant to be a conduit between the AMM/ASC and the other ASEAN bodies. He was also given a limited executive function, viz., to 'initiate plans and programmes of activities for ASEAN regional cooperation in accordance with approved policy guidelines'.[73] It is clear that at the start the Secretary-General was seen more as a secretary than a general. His status was below that of the ministers who comprised the AMM. Since he was a civil servant nominated by the member states, he would often also be junior in rank to the members of the ASC.

---

[71] 1985 Protocol Amending the Agreement on Establishment of the ASEAN Secretariat, adopted by the Foreign Ministers at the Eighteenth AMM in Kuala Lumpur on 9 July 1985. At the following Nineteenth AMM in Manila (June 1986) the Foreign Ministers appointed Roderick Yong Yin Fatt of Brunei as Secretary-General for three years commencing on 16 July 1986. He was followed by one other before the 1992 enhancement of the Secretary-General's position, viz., Rusli Noor of Indonesia.

[72] 1976 Agreement on Establishment of the ASEAN Secretariat, Article 3(2)(iii)(a).

[73] Ibid., Article 3(2)(viii).

1.2 ASEAN FROM ITS FOUNDING

The role of the Secretary-General was enhanced in 1992 and his term of office extended to five years.[74] He was re-designated as Secretary-General of ASEAN and accorded ministerial status.[75] The Secretary-General's job was, inter alia, to 'initiate, advise [sic], co-ordinate and implement ASEAN activities'[76] and to 'offer assessments and recommendations on ASEAN's external relations' to the AMM.[77] He was specifically charged with monitoring the Agreement on the CEPT Scheme for the ASEAN Free Trade Area (AFTA) and was made a member of the AFTA Council.[78] Later on he also became a member of the ASEAN Investment Area Council.[79] It was clear that there was a desire that the Secretary-General should play a bigger role in ASEAN as an organisation and not just function as

---

[74] 1992 Protocol Amending the Agreement on Establishment of the ASEAN Secretariat, adopted by the Foreign Ministers at the Twenty-fifth AMM in Manila on 22 July 1992. It came into force on 8 August 1992.

[75] 1976 Agreement on Establishment of the ASEAN Secretariat, Article 3(1) as amended by the 1992 Protocol. See para. 8 of the Singapore Declaration, issued after the Fourth ASEAN Summit on 28 January 1992. The first Secretary-General appointed to the enhanced post was Ajit Singh (Malaysia). He was followed by Rodolfo Severino (Philippines) and Ong Keng Yong (Singapore). All were diplomats before their stints as ASEAN Secretary-General.

[76] 1976 Agreement on Establishment of the ASEAN Secretariat, Article 3(1)(4) as amended by the 1992 Protocol.

[77] 1976 Agreement on Establishment of the ASEAN Secretariat, Article 3(1)(6)(c) as amended by the 1992 Protocol.

[78] 1976 Agreement on Establishment of the ASEAN Secretariat, Article 3(1)(6)(h) as amended by the 1992 Protocol and the 1992 Agreement on the Common Effective Preferential Tariff (CEPT) Scheme for the ASEAN Free Trade Area, Article 7.

[79] 1998 Framework Agreement on the ASEAN Investment Area, Article 16.

the head of the Secretariat. The Secretary-General of ASEAN was supposed to be ASEAN's public face, in his capacity as spokesman and representative of ASEAN.[80] Since he attended all the Summits, the AMM and the AEM as well as other meetings, he would effectively be the one person who had a bird's-eye view of all the increasingly multifarious activities of ASEAN.

The initial organisation of the Secretariat was very modest: three bureau directors, a foreign trade and economic relations officer, an administrative officer, a public relations officer and an assistant to the Secretary-General.[81] All of these personnel were to be nominated by the member states and appointed by the ASC for a term of three years, which could be renewed. In terms of diplomatic rank the bureau directors rated as counsellors while the others were to be of at least first secretary level. It was envisaged that these officers might be seconded from the Home Service of a member state, as it was explicitly provided that secondment would not affect seniority or promotional prospects in the Home Service. Locally recruited staff would fill clerical and other junior posts.[82] ASEC's budget and the salaries of the political appointees were to be approved by the AMM.[83]

---

[80] 1976 Agreement on Establishment of the ASEAN Secretariat, Article 3(1)(5)(a) as amended by the 1992 Protocol.

[81] 1976 Agreement on Establishment of the ASEAN Secretariat, Article 4(1). In 1983 provision was made for more political appointees, as determined by the ASC; see the 1983 Protocol Amending the Agreement on Establishment of the ASEAN Secretariat.

[82] 1976 Agreement on Establishment of the ASEAN Secretariat, Article 5.

[83] Ibid., Articles 7 and 9. Effectively, the ASC would have had oversight since they would prepare the recommendations for the AMM.

1.2 ASEAN FROM ITS FOUNDING

In 1989 ASEC was reorganised and the post of Deputy Secretary-General (DSG) was introduced.[84] Like the Secretary-General, the DSG's post was rotated among the member states in alphabetical order. To provide continuity, the DSG's appointment would overlap with the incoming and outgoing Secretaries-General. It was explicitly provided that the DSG should be from the public service of the nominating member state. In diplomatic terms he ranked as minister or minister-counsellor. The function of the DSG was, inter alia, to coordinate the research activities of ASEC and handle matters pertaining to ASEAN-affiliated NGOs.[85] Nine assistant directors were provided for in addition to the three bureau directors. It was also explicitly stated that the bureau directors and assistant directors should be from the public service of the nominating state.[86]

The 1992 reorganisation of ASEC added another bureau director, two more assistant directors and eight senior officers, a recognition of the increased demands on the Secretariat. Hitherto, the DSG, bureau directors and assistant directors had been politically appointed.[87] They were now

---

[84] 1989 Protocol Amending the Agreement on Establishment of the ASEAN Secretariat, adopted at the Twenty-second AMM in Bandar Seri Begawan, Brunei (4 July 1989). Dr Chng Meng Kng of Singapore was appointed by the Twenty-third AMM in July 1990.

[85] Article 5 of the 1976 Agreement on Establishment of the ASEAN Secretariat as amended by the 1989 Protocol.

[86] Article 4 of the 1976 Agreement on Establishment of the ASEAN Secretariat as amended by the 1989 Protocol.

[87] 1976 Agreement on Establishment of the ASEAN Secretariat, Article 4. The subsequent amending Protocols did not change this system of political appointments.

33

designated as openly recruited staff in an attempt to professionalise the Secretariat.[88] Although the professional staff were supposed to be openly recruited on the basis of merit, there was to be a quota system to ensure representation of all member countries in ASEC.[89] A further expansion of the Secretariat was authorised in 1997, with the creation of a second DSG post.[90] In a retrograde step, the 1997 amendment Protocol provided that the two DSGs should be nominated by member states.[91] The DSG posts were rotated in alphabetical order, so that at any one time three member states would have nominees at the apex of ASEC. Thus, until the coming into force of the ASEAN Charter in December 2008 the Secretariat consisted of the politically appointed Secretary-General and his two DSGs, supported by professional staff openly recruited from the ASEAN member states as well as locally recruited junior staff.

The Secretariat was precisely that: a Secretariat and not an independent institution capable of political action. However, ASEC was increasingly entrusted with the role of monitoring compliance with ASEAN agreements, especially the economic ones. Under the Framework Agreement on Enhancing ASEAN Economic Cooperation 1992 ASEC was

---

[88] 1976 Agreement on Establishment of the ASEAN Secretariat, Article 4 as amended by the 1992 Protocol.

[89] Para. 8 of the Singapore Declaration (January 1992).

[90] 1997 Protocol Amending the Agreement on Establishment of the ASEAN Secretariat, adopted by the Foreign Ministers at the Thirtieth AMM in Subang Jaya, Malaysia on 23 July 1997.

[91] 1976 Agreement on Establishment of the ASEAN Secretariat, Article 4(2) as amended by the 1997 Protocol.

1.2 ASEAN FROM ITS FOUNDING

given the task of monitoring the progress of any arrangements arising from the agreement.[92] Similarly, under the Agreement on CEPT Scheme for the ASEAN Free Trade Area 1992 ASEC was to monitor the implementation of the agreement, reporting to SEOM.[93] The ASEAN Framework Agreement on Goods in Transit 1998 created a Transit Transport Coordinating Board including a representative of ASEC.[94] ASEC was to submit evaluation reports to the Board for further action. Under the 2004 ASEAN Framework Agreement for Integration of Priority Sectors ASEC was again required to submit reports to SEOM on the implementation of the agreement.[95] ASEC was also given the role of providing secretarial support to the many bodies that were formed pursuant to ASEAN agreements, not only amongst the member states but also with external partners.[96]

---

[92] 1992 Framework Agreement on Enhancing ASEAN Economic Cooperation, Article 7.
[93] Agreement on the Common Effective Preferential Tariff (CEPT) Scheme for the ASEAN Free Trade Area, Article 7(3).
[94] 1998 Framework Agreement on Facilitation of Goods in Transit, Article 29.
[95] 2004 ASEAN Framework Agreement for Integration of Priority Sectors, Article 19.
[96] See, e.g., the Framework Agreement on Comprehensive Economic Cooperation between India and ASEAN and China (2002), Article 12; Framework Agreement on Comprehensive Economic Cooperation between India and ASEAN (2003), Article 12; Framework Agreement for Comprehensive Economic Partnership between Japan and ASEAN (2003), Article 11; Framework Agreement on Comprehensive Economic Cooperation among the Governments of Member Countries of ASEAN and the Republic of Korea (2005), Article 5.4.

The demands on ASEC have expanded exponentially since its creation in 1976. ASEC not only provided secretarial support for ASEAN meetings, it was tasked with a host of monitoring functions under the many agreements entered into by ASEAN member states. Together, ASEC and the Secretary-General formed a neutral centre in ASEAN affairs and provided the institutional memory of the organisation. When the pace of ASEAN integration quickened during the first decade of the twenty-first century the number of meetings rose considerably. More and more tasks were given to ASEC with each new agreement. On the eve of the adoption of the ASEAN Charter just keeping track of the burgeoning number of initiatives and agreements was becoming a problem.

(1.2.2.4) Other ministerial bodies

Apart from the AMM and AEM, other ministries began meeting on a regular basis under the ASEAN umbrella. This has led to a veritable alphabet soup of acronyms. The first meeting of ASEAN Labour Ministers (ALMM) took place in Jakarta in April 1975, continuing roughly on a biannual basis thereafter.[97] A meeting of the ASEAN Education Ministers (ASED) was first held in 1977 in Manila; however, ASED only met intermittently thereafter.[98] In 1979 the first Meeting of the ASEAN Ministers of Agriculture and Forestry (AMAF) took place in Manila to issue the ASEAN Food Security Reserve

---

[97] The last such meeting, the Twenty-first ALMM, was held in Hanoi, Vietnam, in May 2010.
[98] The Seventh ASED only took place in July 2012 in Yogyakarta, Indonesia.

1.2 ASEAN FROM ITS FOUNDING

Agreement.[99] ASEAN Ministers of Health at their First Meeting (AHMM) held in July 1980 in Manila adopted the Declaration on Collaboration in Health to strengthen and coordinate regional cooperation in health among ASEAN countries.[100] In October the same year the first ASEAN Ministerial Meeting on Science and Technology (AMMST) took place in Pattaya, Thailand.[101] Also in 1980 the ASEAN Ministers on Energy Meeting (AMEM) was held for the first time in Bali.[102] The environmental ministers met for the first ASEAN Ministerial Meeting on the Environment (AMME) in Manila in 1981 to issue an ASEAN Declaration on the Environment.[103] The ALAWMM was established in 1986, to be held every thirty-six months thereafter with Senior Law Officials' Meetings (ASLOMs) in between.[104] In 1989 a Conference of ASEAN Ministers Responsible for Information (AMRI) was inaugurated.[105]

---

[99] Thereafter, the meetings have taken place annually, the Thirty-fourth AMAF being held in Vientiane, Laos, in September 2012.

[100] This meets every two years, the last meeting being the Tenth AHMM in Singapore on 22 July 2012. Curiously, there appears to have been an Eleventh AHMM in Phuket, Thailand, on 6 July 2012.

[101] The Fourteenth AMMST was held in Ho Chi Minh City, Vietnam, in November 2011.

[102] This has been held quite regularly, the Thirtieth AMEM being in Phnom Penh, Cambodia, in September 2012.

[103] The last meeting, the Eleventh AMME, was held in Singapore in October 2009.

[104] The Eighth ALAWMM took place in Phnom Penh, Cambodia, in November 2011.

[105] This meets irregularly, the Eleventh AMRI being held in Kuala Lumpur, Malaysia, in March 2012.

The last decade of the twentieth century saw the establishment of more ASEAN Ministerial Meetings. The ASEAN Transport Ministers' Meeting (ATM) was held for the first time in 1996, and annually thereafter.[106] The Finance Ministers started meeting in 1997 (AFMM) after the leaders had directed that there should be greater economic integration.[107] In December 1997 the Ministers of the Interior or Home Affairs of the ASEAN member states issued the ASEAN Declaration on Transnational Crime at the first ASEAN Conference on Transnational Crime in Manila. This was a result of the Twenty-ninth AMM the previous year, which called for greater cooperation in combating transnational crime like the drug trade, money laundering and illegal migration, and the subsequent First Informal ASEAN Summit in Jakarta. The Declaration established the ASEAN Ministerial Meeting on Transnational Crime (AMMTC)[108] to coordinate the activities of ASEAN bodies like the ASEAN Senior Officials on Drug Matters (ASOD) and the meeting of ASEAN Chiefs of National Police (ASEANAPOL). The following year saw the establishment of the ASEAN Tourism Ministers' Meeting (M-ATM).[109] The M-ATM supervises the ASEAN Tourism Agreement of 2002.[110] The year 1998 also

[106] The Eighteenth ATM took place in Bali, Indonesia, in November 2012.
[107] The ministers have been meeting annually, the Sixteenth AFMM being held in Phnom Penh, Cambodia, in March 2012.
[108] The AMMTC meets every two years, the Eighth AMMTC having been held in Bali, Indonesia, in October 2011.
[109] Tourism is one of the priority sectors for ASEAN integration. The Fifteenth M-ATM took place in Manado, Indonesia, in January 2012.
[110] Article 9 of the ASEAN Tourism Agreement 2002, signed in Phnom Penh at the Eighth ASEAN Summit.

1.2 ASEAN FROM ITS FOUNDING

saw an informal meeting of ASEAN Ministers on Rural Development and Poverty Eradication (AMRDPE) against the backdrop of the financial crisis. Thereafter, the ministers met on an irregular basis to discuss poverty eradication.[111]

To round up, in the new millennium the following meetings were established: the ASEAN Telecommunications and IT Ministers' Meeting (TELMIN) in 2001;[112] the meeting of ASEAN Ministers Responsible for Culture and the Arts (AMCA) in 2003;[113] the ASEAN Ministerial Meeting on Minerals (AMMin) in 2005;[114] and the ASEAN Defence Ministers' Meeting (ADMM) in 2006.[115]

It will be seen that by the time the Eleventh ASEAN Summit took place in Kuala Lumpur in December 2005 the web of links among ministries in the ASEAN member states had spread to practically all fields. The foregoing list is not exhaustive, even regarding ministerial-level meetings; there are dozens of other meetings, both formal as well as informal, at all levels. There was a pressing need for some sort of coordination mechanism to pull together all the strands of

---

[111] The Seventh AMRDPE took place in Bandar Seri Begawan, Brunei, in November 2011.

[112] This meets annually. The Eleventh TELMIN was held in Nay Pyi Taw, Myanmar, in December 2011.

[113] Meetings have not been regular. The Fourth AMCA took place in Pampanga, Philippines in March 2010.

[114] This is supposed to meet at least once in three years. There have only been three meetings, the Third AMMin being held in Hanoi, Vietnam, in December 2011.

[115] This meets annually. The Sixth ADMM took place in Phnom Penh, Cambodia, in May 2012.

ASEAN cooperation. Thus, the leaders issued the Kuala Lumpur Declaration on the Establishment of the ASEAN Charter. The aim was to formalise the institutional framework of ASEAN and to clothe it with legal personality.

1.3 The ASEAN Charter and beyond

The quick survey in the foregoing section of the landscape after the Eleventh ASEAN Summit would have revealed the ad hoc and piecemeal way in which ASEAN institutions developed. All too often it seemed that having a fine document as a 'deliverable' after a ministerial meeting was what mattered, not the substance or implementation of the commitments undertaken. ASEAN had been driven primarily by the foreign ministries, with the economic ministries forging ahead on a separate course. By 2003 it was felt by some forward thinkers at the foreign ministries that ASEAN needed a grand plan to chart its way in the twenty-first century.

1.3.1 *The road to the Charter*

The idea of a Charter for ASEAN was floated as early as 1974 at the Seventh AMM in Jakarta.[116] Mr Carlos Romulo, the Secretary of Foreign Affairs of the Philippines, advanced a proposal for a Charter in order to 'institutionalise the function and structure of ASEAN'. The other members were not enthusiastic and referred the matter to the ASC, where the idea languished for two decades. At the Kuala Lumpur informal Summit

---

[116] Joint Communiqué of the Seventh AMM (Jakarta, May 1974), para. 9.

1.3 THE ASEAN CHARTER AND BEYOND

in December 1996 a Vision 2020 was promulgated on the occasion of the thirtieth anniversary of ASEAN. This Vision 2020 pledged the creation of 'a stable, prosperous and highly competitive ASEAN Economic Region in which there is a free flow of goods, services and investments, a freer flow of capital, equitable economic development and reduced poverty and socio-economic disparities' by the year 2020. Shortly after that the economic crisis hit ASEAN badly, severely damaging the regional economies. There was a political crisis in Indonesia, which led to the fall of President Soeharto and fears that the country might break up. The economic crisis of 1997 caused ASEAN's share of world GDP to fall from a peak of 4.2 percent to 3.9 percent in 1998,[117] and its share of world trade declined from 6.5 percent in 1997 to 5.5 percent in 1998.[118] The fall in ASEAN's share of world inward foreign direct investment flows was even more drastic: from 7 percent in 1997 to 3.1 percent in 1998, to a low of 1.7 percent in 2000.[119] In the meantime, China and, later, India were posing increasing competition to ASEAN, which until 1997 had been on the economic upswing.

Indonesia and ASEAN survived the economic and political crisis of 1997, but it was a severe jolt to the self-congratulatory mood in which the thirtieth anniversary was celebrated. It was in a more sober frame of mind that the Sixth ASEAN Summit in Hanoi (December 1998) saw the launch of the Hanoi Action Plan to realise the Vision 2020. The Hanoi

---

[117] Wong Poh Kam and Ng Kwan Kee, *The Competitiveness of ASEAN after the 1997 Asian Financial Crisis* (Asia Competitiveness Institute Monograph Series, Singapore, August 1998), table 5.
[118] Ibid., table 7.   [119] Ibid., table 21.

Action Plan envisaged a host of measures to strengthen macroeconomic and financial cooperation and enhance economic integration. Both the AMM and AEM were involved in implementing the measures. A Special Joint Ministerial Meeting (JMM) among Economic, Finance and Foreign Ministers was convened at the Third Informal Summit (Manila, 1999) to discuss cross-sectoral coordination to aid the regional recovery process.[120] In 2001, following up from an idea mooted at the AEM Retreat in Siem Reap, Cambodia, the Ministers agreed to commission a reputable international consultant to conduct an ASEAN Competitiveness Study.[121]

The interim report by McKinsey & Company was presented to the ASEAN leaders at the Eighth ASEAN Summit in Phnom Penh (November 2002) and the final report was completed the following year. This report was considered by the High Level Task Force (HLTF) on ASEAN Economic Integration in formulating its recommendations. At the Thirty-fifth AEM in Phnom Penh in September 2003, the Economic Ministers approved the recommendation of the HLTF on ASEAN Economic Integration to formalise the ASEAN Economic Community (AEC) as the end-goal of ASEAN economic integration. ASEAN would become a single market and production base by 2020, characterised by the free flow of goods, services, investment and skilled labour and a freer flow of capital.[122]

---

[120] Joint Press Statement of the Thirty-first AEM in Singapore, 30 September 1999, para. 39.
[121] Joint Press Statement of the Thirty-third ASEAN Economic Ministers' Meeting (Hanoi, 15 September 2001), para. 12.
[122] Joint Press Statement of the Thirty-fifth ASEAN Economic Ministers' Meeting (Phnom Penh, 4 September 2003), para. 15.

1.3 THE ASEAN CHARTER AND BEYOND

Subsequently, the deadline for the establishment of the ASEAN community was accelerated to 2015 at the Twelfth ASEAN Summit (Cebu, Philippines, January 2007).[123]

It was against this backdrop that the Ninth ASEAN Summit adopted Bali Concord II in October 2003.[124] Bali Concord II stated that an ASEAN Community would be established consisting of three pillars, viz., political and security cooperation, economic cooperation and socio-cultural cooperation. The ASEAN Political-Security Community (APSC)[125] was not meant to coordinate the foreign or defence policies of the member states. Indeed, it was explicitly recognised that member states had a 'sovereign right' to pursue individual foreign policies and defence arrangements. What was envisaged was closer cooperation in the political-security field.[126] Similarly, the ASEAN Socio-Cultural Community

---

[123] See the Cebu Declaration on the Acceleration of the Establishment of an ASEAN Community (January 2007).

[124] Declaration of ASEAN Concord II (Bali Concord II), signed by the leaders of the ASEAN member states in Bali, 7 October 2003.

[125] This is referred to in Bali Concord II as the ASEAN Security Community, abbreviated to ASC. It was later realised that the acronym ASC had already been used for the ASEAN Standing Community. In the ASEAN Charter the ASEAN Security Community was redesignated as the ASEAN Political and Security Community or APSC. To avoid confusion, the abbreviation APSC will be used henceforward when referring to the (then) ASEAN Security Community.

[126] In November 2011 the leaders issued a Bali Declaration on ASEAN Community in a Global Community of Nations (Bali Concord III), in which they adopted 'an ASEAN common platform on global issues'. This is meant to ensure a 'more coordinated, cohesive and coherent ASEAN position on global issues of common interest and concern ... which would further enhance ASEAN's common voice in relevant

(ASCC) was meant to foster social development and cultural cooperation. The meat was in the ASEAN Economic Community (AEC). The AEC envisaged economic integration of the economies of the member states by 2020. Integration meant creating a single market and production base. The development gap between the older members and the CLMV countries would be bridged. Significantly, Bali Concord II called for the improvement of the existing dispute settlement mechanism (DSM) to 'ensure expeditious and legally binding resolution of any economic disputes'. The recommendations of the HLTF on ASEAN economic integration were annexed. The HLTF recommended (inter alia) the setting up of a legal unit within ASEC to provide advice on trade disputes, a consultative body to resolve operational problems, a compliance body to adjudicate and a dispute settlement mechanism.[127]

In September 2004 the AEM noted that a legal unit had been set up in ASEC. The ASEAN Consultation to Solve Trade and Investment Issues (ACT) and the ASEAN Compliance Body (ACB) had also been established.[128] The Protocol on Enhanced Dispute Settlement Mechanism was adopted by the Economic Ministers at the Tenth ASEAN Summit (Vientiane, Laos, November 2004). The Tenth Summit also saw the

---

multilateral fora'. This presages a more coordinated approach to political and security cooperation. The common platform is to be realised by 2022.

[127] Recommendations of the High Level Task Force on ASEAN Economic Integration, para. 14.

[128] Joint Press Statement of the Thirty-sixth ASEAN Economic Ministers' Meeting (Jakarta, September 2004), para. 15.

1.3 THE ASEAN CHARTER AND BEYOND

signing of the Vientiane Action Programme (VAP) by the leaders. This replaced the Hanoi Plan of Action. The VAP was a six-year plan designed to deepen economic integration and narrow the development gap between the older members and the CLMV countries. A Framework Agreement for Integration of Priority Sectors was also signed. In addition, the ASEAN Socio-Cultural Community Plan of Action and the ASEAN Security Community Plan of Action were adopted. Buried in the Annex to the latter was a commitment to work towards the development of an ASEAN Charter,

> which will inter alia reaffirm ASEAN's goals and principles in inter-state relations, in particular the collective responsibilities of all ASEAN Member Countries in ensuring non-aggression and respect for each other's sovereignty and territorial integrity; the promotion and protection of human rights; the maintenance of political stability, regional peace and economic progress; and the establishment of effective and efficient institutional framework for ASEAN.[129]

In fact, Malaysia had already proposed to reform the institutional framework of ASEAN at the FMM retreat in Ha Long Bay, Vietnam, in March 2004. It was recognised that the existing regime was political rather than legal. There was a lack of coordination, which could only get worse with the proliferation of ASEAN bodies and meetings. The following year, the AMM agreed to work towards the promulgation of an ASEAN Charter which would 'reaffirm the objectives,

---

[129] Annex to the ASEAN Security Community Plan of Action 2004, para. II.2.

goals and principles of the ASEAN Community'.[130] Reforming the institutional framework was a principal goal. The ASEAN leaders issued the Declaration on the Establishment of the ASEAN Charter at the Eleventh ASEAN Summit held in Kuala Lumpur (December 2005). The declared aim of the Charter was to create the legal and institutional framework for ASEAN, which had hitherto been functioning on a totally informal basis. The Charter was also meant to 'codify all ASEAN norms, rules and values' and confer legal personality on ASEAN. To this end, an Eminent Persons' Group (EPG) was set up and tasked with re-imagining ASEAN as an organisation.[131] The EPG was enjoined to 'put forward bold and visionary recommendations' as well as undertake a thorough review of the ASEAN institutional framework and propose improvements.[132] Apart from institutional streamlining,

---

[130] Joint Communiqué of the Thirty-eighth AMM (Vientiane, July 2005), para. 6.

[131] The EPG consisted of the following: Pehin Dato Lim Jock Seng (Minister of Foreign Affairs and Trade II, Brunei); Dr Aun Porn Moniroth (Advisor to the Prime Minister and Chairman of the Supreme National Economic Council, Cambodia); Mr Ali Alatas (former Minister of Foreign Affairs, Indonesia); Mr Kamphan Simmalavong (former Deputy Minister, Laos); Tan Sri Musa Hitam (former Deputy Prime Minister, Malaysia); Dr Than Nyun (Chairman of the Civil Service Selection and Training Board, Myanmar); Mr Fidel Ramos (former President, Philippines); Professor S. Jayakumar (Deputy Prime Minister, Singapore); Mr Kasemsamosorn Kasemsri (former Deputy Prime Minister and Minister of Foreign Affairs, Thailand); Mr Nguyen Manh Cam (former Deputy Prime Minister and Minister of Foreign Affairs, Vietnam).

[132] Terms of Reference of the Eminent Persons' Group on the ASEAN Charter, para. 3.

1.3 THE ASEAN CHARTER AND BEYOND

the EPG was specifically asked to look into effective conflict resolution mechanisms.[133] The Secretary-General was to brief the EPG on ASEAN issues. Two senior staff members of ASEC were assigned as resource persons. The EPG was given a year to report.

The EPG held extensive consultations with ASEAN stakeholders, including the ASEAN Inter-Parliamentary Organisation (AIPO), Working Group for an ASEAN Human Rights Mechanism, ASEAN Institutes of Strategic and International Studies (ASEAN-ISIS), civil society organisations, ASEAN Chambers of Commerce and Industry (ASEAN-CCI) and the private sector. The EPG met eight times over the course of the year. They also made a visit to Brussels to study the experience of the EU. Their report was ready for presentation at the Twelfth ASEAN Summit, which was scheduled to be held in Cebu, the Philippines, in December 2006. As it happened the Cebu Summit was postponed on account of a threatened typhoon. It took place finally in January 2007. The Cebu Declaration on the Blueprint for the ASEAN Charter was issued endorsing the Report of the Eminent Persons' Group and setting up a High Level Task Force (HLTF) for Drafting of the ASEAN Charter.[134] The

---

[133] Ibid., para. 4.2(i).
[134] The members of the HLTF were: Pengiran Dato Paduka Osman Patra (Permanent Secretary, Ministry of Foreign Affairs and Trade, Brunei); Dr Kao Kim Hourn (Secretary of State, Ministry of Foreign Affairs and International Cooperation, Cambodia); Mr Dian Triansyah Djani (Director-General, ASEAN-Indonesia, Department of Foreign Affairs, Indonesia); Mr Bounkeut Sangsomsak (Deputy Minister, Ministry of Foreign Affairs, Laos); Tan Sri Ahmad Fuzi Haji Abdul Razak

HLTF was given until November 2007 to finish its task – less than the time the EPG had to formulate its 'bold and visionary' recommendations.

1.3.2 The ASEAN Charter and after

The Eminent Persons' Group (EPG) stated that the ultimate aim was the formation of an ASEAN Union.[135] ASEAN as an organisation should have legal personality.[136] However, the EPG also recognised that ASEAN's main problem was not

---

(Ambassador-at-large, Malaysia); Mr Aung Bwa (Director-General, ASEAN-Myanmar, Ministry of Foreign Affairs, Myanmar); Mrs Rosario Manalo (Special Envoy, Department of Foreign Affairs, Philippines); Professor Tommy Koh (Ambassador-at-large, Singapore) (in addition, Professor Walter Woon (Solicitor-General and Ambassador, Singapore) functioned as alternate member of the HLTF and Singapore delegation leader when Professor Koh took over the Chairmanship of the HLTF from Mrs Manalo); Mr Sihasak Phuangketkeow (Deputy Permanent Secretary, Ministry of Foreign Affairs, Thailand) (Mr Pradap Pibulsonggram (Deputy Permanent Secretary, Ministry of Foreign Affairs, Thailand) replaced Khun Sihasak in March 2007); Mr Nguyan Trung Thanh (Assistant Minister, Ministry of Foreign Affairs, Vietnam).

[135] Report of the Eminent Persons' Group on the ASEAN Charter, para. 23. Although the Report was endorsed by the ASEAN leaders, there was little enthusiasm for the creation of such a Union. This was an initiative of the Philippines. In drafting the Charter, no reference was made to the idea of an ASEAN Union.

[136] Report of the Eminent Persons' Group on the ASEAN Charter, para. 43. See now Article 3 of the ASEAN Charter. The concern of the drafters of the Charter was to make clear that ASEAN was to have a legal personality in the domestic law of the member states.

1.3 THE ASEAN CHARTER AND BEYOND

lack of vision; the main problem was following up on the grand declarations, plans of action and roadmaps. This has been a constant shortcoming identified by the Secretaries-General not only to the EPG but also to the High Level Task Force (HLTF) on Drafting of the ASEAN Charter. It was stated baldly that 'ASEAN must establish a culture of honouring and implementing its decisions and agreements, and carrying them out on time'.[137]

Four particular areas should be highlighted:

(1.3.2.1) Dispute settlement

To remedy the deficiency in carrying out commitments, the EPG recommended the establishment of dispute settlement mechanisms in all fields of ASEAN cooperation, including monitoring and enforcement mechanisms.[138] The ASEAN Secretariat was to be entrusted with monitoring compliance with ASEAN decisions, agreements and action plans. The Secretary-General was to report instances of non-compliance to the ASEAN Summit.[139]

These recommendations were largely implemented when it came to the drafting of the Charter. Some High Level Task Force (HLTF) delegations initially expressed a view that

---

[137] Report of the Eminent Persons' Group on the ASEAN Charter, para. 44. This remains a matter of concern even now; in conversation with one of the authors, this issue was repeatedly raised by ASEAN officials and former Secretaries-General.

[138] Report of the Eminent Persons' Group on the ASEAN Charter, Executive Summary, para. 6.

[139] Report of the Eminent Persons' Group on the ASEAN Charter, para. 45. See now Article 27(1) of the ASEAN Charter.

a court should be set up. This idea was quickly scotched. ASEAN was not ready for a pan-ASEAN judicial institution. Although not explicitly articulated, it was clear that an ASEAN court could not be established as long as the rule of law was weak in some ASEAN states. Any court would have been compromised from the start if a judge had to take instructions from his country. Indeed, far from wanting a court, some member states appeared to be wary of any sort of compulsory adjudication, despite the clear mandate given by the EPG. One can only speculate as to the instructions that these delegations received, but it did appear that their preference was to keep the settlement of disputes on the political plane, to be dealt with by the ASEAN Summit.

The HLTF was conscious that there were existing dispute settlement mechanisms in the TAC and Vientiane Protocol. The decision was taken to use these as the basis for Chapter VIII of the Charter, filling in the gaps as necessary. The scheme of Chapter VIII is thus: the first line in settling a dispute is dialogue, consultation and negotiation.[140] This was a concession to those who had reservations about too much law being involved in the process of dispute settlement. Article 23 then goes on to provide that the parties to the dispute may agree to resort to good offices, conciliation or mediation. These are the voluntary, non-binding modes of settlement favoured by some countries. It is provided that the parties to the dispute may request the Chairman of ASEAN or the Secretary-General to provide good offices, conciliation or mediation.[141]

---

[140] ASEAN Charter, Article 22(1).   [141] Ibid., Article 23(2).

1.3 THE ASEAN CHARTER AND BEYOND

Where a specific ASEAN instrument provides for dispute settlement, the mechanisms and procedures set out should be utilised.[142] The main weakness of this is that the dispute settlement 'mechanism' in some ASEAN instruments will most likely prove ineffective in resolving disputes. For example, the 2002 ASEAN Agreement on Transboundary Haze Pollution provides that disputes will be settled amicably by consultation or negotiation,[143] which hardly inspires confidence that problems will be resolved in a legally binding manner.

The mechanism in the Treaty of Amity and Cooperation in Southeast Asia (TAC) is to be used to resolve disputes that do not involve the interpretation or application of any ASEAN instrument.[144] Again, the primary problem with the TAC is that the dispute settlement mechanism is voluntary. There is no means to force an unwilling party to settle a dispute under the TAC. This is discussed in more detail in the next chapter.

Finally, where there is no specific provision, disputes concerning ASEAN economic agreements are to be settled in accordance with the Vientiane Protocol on the Enhanced Dispute Settlement Mechanism.[145] This is one of the most crucial provisions in the Charter. The creation of an ASEAN community will be driven by economic integration. This was explicitly

---

[142] Ibid., Article 24(1).
[143] See Article 27 of the Treaty, which was signed in Kuala Lumpur on 10 June 2002. It has been ratified by all ASEAN member states save Indonesia, from which the haze principally originates.
[144] ASEAN Charter, Article 24(2).   [145] Ibid., Article 24(3).

ASEAN AS AN ORGANISATION

recognised by the EPG in its report.[146] Economic integration cannot happen without some means of binding dispute settlement. Hence the push for the creation of an effective dispute settlement mechanism in the economic field. The Vientiane Protocol was meant to ensure that legally binding decisions could be made and expeditiously enforced,[147] a vital prerequisite for the creation of an economic community.

Any party affected by non-compliance with the result of a dispute settlement process may refer the matter to the Summit for a decision.[148] Unresolved disputes also go to the Summit for decision.[149] In time to come, the ASEAN Summit may evolve into a kind of final tribunal of appeal from dispute settlement bodies. If and when this happens, it would be imperative to ensure that the decisions of the Summit are firmly rooted in law if ASEAN is to be taken seriously as a rules-based organisation adhering to the rule of law.[150]

(1.3.2.2) The Community Councils

A major institutional reform was the creation of three ministerial councils to oversee the three pillars of the ASEAN

---

[146] See paras. 14–15 of the Report of the Eminent Persons' Group on the ASEAN Charter.
[147] See the Joint Media Statement of the Thirty-sixth AEM (Jakarta, September 2004), paras. 9–11.
[148] ASEAN Charter, Article 27(2).   [149] Ibid., Article 26.
[150] The latest reiteration of this is to be found in Bali Concord III (signed by the ASEAN leaders in November 2011) where it is stated that the ASEAN common platform on global issues is to be based on 'a strengthened ASEAN Community centred on ASEAN as a rules-based organisation, with the ASEAN Charter as the foundation'.

1.3 THE ASEAN CHARTER AND BEYOND

Community.[151] This was to meet the challenge of dealing with transnational and trans-sectoral issues. Until the promulgation of the Charter, ASEAN ministerial bodies had tended to meet in isolation from other such bodies. In the Report of the Eminent Persons' Group the example of avian influenza was given, an issue which involved the Health and Agriculture Ministers as well as the immigration authorities.[152] Article 9(1) of the Charter creates the ASEAN Political-Security Community Council (APSC), the ASEAN Economic Community Council (AECC) and the Socio-Cultural Community Council (ASCC). Each Community Council had under its purview the relevant ASEAN sectoral ministerial bodies listed in Annex 1 of the Charter. The APSC thus had the AMM under its wing, as well as five other sectoral bodies. The AECC oversees the AEM and thirteen other sectoral bodies. The ASCC is the most diverse, taking care of everything else that does not fall within the purview of the APSC and AECC. Seventeen sectoral ministerial bodies are listed. The aim of the three councils is to coordinate the work of the different sectors and ensure the implementation of the decisions of the ASEAN Summit.[153]

The AECC is the most developed of the three councils, which is unsurprising given that economic integration is now the main driving force behind ASEAN. The leaders adopted the ASEAN Economic Community Blueprint at the Thirteenth Summit at the same time as the Charter was

---

[151] Report of the Eminent Persons' Group on the ASEAN Charter, Executive Summary, para. 4.
[152] Report of the Eminent Persons' Group on the ASEAN Charter, para. 35.
[153] ASEAN Charter, Article 9(4).

ASEAN AS AN ORGANISATION

signed. It was meant to serve as a roadmap for the transformation of ASEAN into a single market and production base by 2015.[154] The key characteristic of the AEC was declared to be 'adherence to rules-based systems for effective compliance and [implementation] of economic commitments'.[155] The ASEAN single market and production base comprises five elements: (i) free flow of goods; (ii) free flow of services; (iii) free flow of investments; (iv) freer flow of capital; and (v) free flow of skilled labour.[156] There are numerous references throughout the Blueprint to the harmonisation and coordination of policies across ASEAN. The implementation of the Blueprint is entrusted to the various sectoral ministerial bodies under the aegis of the AEM, who are in charge of economic integration in the AECC.[157]

The APSC is helmed by the Foreign Ministers. The ASEAN Political-Security Community Blueprint was adopted at the Fourteenth ASEAN Summit in March 2009. This Blueprint also envisages a 'rules-based community of shared values and norms'.[158] The primary aim is to maintain peace in the region. The emphasis is on the renunciation of the use of force and reliance on peaceful settlement of disputes.[159] Recognising the deficiencies of the dispute settlement mechanisms, the Blueprint requires that the existing mechanisms be enhanced.[160] In addition to peace and security, law and

---

[154] Chairman's Statement of the Thirteenth ASEAN Summit (Singapore, November 2007), para. 8.
[155] ASEAN Economic Community Blueprint, para. 5.   [156] Ibid., para. 9.
[157] Ibid., para. 70.   [158] Ibid., para. 10.   [159] Ibid., para. 9.
[160] Ibid., para. B.2.1.

1.3 THE ASEAN CHARTER AND BEYOND

order are also in the forefront of the APSC. ASEAN member states committed themselves to combating transnational crime, trafficking in persons and dealing in illicit drugs and to fighting piracy and terrorism.[161] These goals were reiterated in the Bali Declaration on ASEAN Community in a Global Community of Nations (Bali Concord III).[162] Bali Concord III also commits the member states to intensifying cooperation to combat corruption.[163]

The APSC Blueprint also specifically committed ASEAN to the establishment of a human rights body. This was done in October 2009 at the Fifteenth ASEAN Summit.[164] The ASEAN Intergovernmental Commission on Human Rights (AICHR) held its first meeting at the ASEAN Secretariat in April 2010. One of its major tasks was to develop an ASEAN Human Rights Declaration (AHRD).[165] The first meeting of the AICHR on the AHRD was held in January 2012 in Siem Reap, Cambodia. The AHRD was adopted by the ASEAN leaders at the Twenty-first ASEAN Summit in Phnom Penh, Cambodia, in November 2012.

Of the three Community Councils, the ASCC is the most amorphous. It covers all the areas of ASEAN cooperation not dealt with by the AECC and APSC. As one might

---

[161] Ibid., paras. B.4.1 and B.4.2.
[162] Signed in Bali by the ASEAN leaders in November 2011.
[163] Bali Concord III, para. A.1.j.
[164] Cha-Am Hua Hin Declaration on the Intergovernmental Commission on Human Rights, issued by the ASEAN leaders at the Fifteenth ASEAN Summit, 23 October 2009.
[165] Terms of Reference of the ASEAN Intergovernmental Commission on Human Rights, para. 4.2.

expect, there is also an ASEAN Blueprint for the ASEAN Socio-Cultural Community.[166] This covers such diverse matters as education, human resource development, information and communications technology, poverty alleviation, social safety nets, food security and safety, health care, rights of migrant workers and environmental sustainability. The aim is to create a 'people-centred' ASEAN community and foster an ASEAN identity.

Coordination of the activities of the three Community Councils to ensure policy coherence, efficiency and cooperation is the job of the ASEAN Coordinating Council (ACC).[167] This comprises the Foreign Ministers and meets twice a year to prepare the way for the Summits.[168] In practice, however, the other Community Councils do not defer to the ACC. Policy coherence is maintained by the leaders themselves at the Summit level. The ASEAN Summit was supposed to have been redesignated as the ASEAN Council on the recommendation of the EPG, but at the Charter-drafting stage it was felt that there was no need to create yet another council. The decision was taken to keep the old familiar nomenclature for the apex organ of ASEAN. The term 'ASEAN Summit' is therefore used to designate both the supreme policy-making organ of ASEAN as well as the meetings of the heads of state and government.[169]

---

[166] Adopted at the Fourteenth ASEAN Summit (Cha-Am, Thailand, March 2009).
[167] ASEAN Charter, Article 8(2).   [168] Ibid., Article 8(1).
[169] Ibid., Article 7.

1.3 THE ASEAN CHARTER AND BEYOND

At the Fourteenth ASEAN Summit in Cha-am, Thailand, in March 2009 the leaders issued a Declaration on the Roadmap for the ASEAN Community (2009–15). This Roadmap adopted the three Community Blueprints and the Initiative for ASEAN Integration Workplan 2, replacing the Vientiane Action Programme.[170] In 2011 the leaders issued a Declaration on 'ASEAN Community in a Global Community of Nations' (Bali Concord III). Bali Concord III pledged the creation of a common ASEAN platform on global issues, though what this might actually mean in practice remains to be seen. This common platform is to be realised by 2022. The ACC was given the coordinating role in this endeavour. The peaceful settlement of disputes in accordance with international law was again emphasised.

(1.3.2.3) The Secretary-General and ASEAN Secretariat

In the Report of the Eminent Persons' Group it was envisaged that the Secretary-General was to be a personage of some significance and take on a greater role, being empowered to sign 'non-sensitive' agreements on behalf of the member states and representing ASEAN at UN and other regional and international forums.[171] He had already been conferred ministerial status as early as 1992,[172] a situation confirmed by the Charter.[173] There was, however, some ambivalence on the

---

[170] Declaration on the Roadmap for the ASEAN Community (2009–15), paras. 1 and 2.
[171] Report of the Eminent Persons' Group on the ASEAN Charter, para. 36.
[172] 1976 Agreement on Establishment of the ASEAN Secretariat, Article 3(1) as amended by the 1992 Protocol.
[173] ASEAN Charter, Article 7(2)(g).

ASEAN AS AN ORGANISATION

part of some of the delegations negotiating the wording of the Charter regarding the question of how independent the Secretary-General could or should be. It was clear that the member states intended to keep control of the ASEAN Secretariat and not allow it to evolve into anything resembling the European Commission. Hence, it is explicitly provided that the Secretary-General is the Chief Administrative Officer of ASEAN,[174] rather than the Chief Executive Officer. The implication is that the Secretary-General oversees the administration of ASEAN and has no independent executive power.

This is abundantly clear when one examines the Blueprints for the three Communities. The Secretary-General of ASEAN is to report the progress of the AEC[175] and ASCC[176] to relevant ministerial meetings and the Summit. The progress of the APSC Blueprint is to be reported to the Summit annually.[177] Under the Roadmap for the ASEAN Community (2009–15), the Secretary-General is also tasked with mobilising resources from the member states, dialogue and sectoral partners, development partners and other external parties.[178] The Secretary-General along with the concerned ASEAN sectoral ministerial bodies is responsible for implementation of the Roadmap.[179] Nowhere is the Secretary-General given an independent right of action, not even when offering good

[174] Ibid., Article 11(3).
[175] ASEAN Economic Community Blueprint, para. 71.
[176] ASEAN Socio-Cultural Community Blueprint, para. III.A.4.
[177] ASEAN Political-Security Community Blueprint, para. 32.
[178] Declaration on the Roadmap for the ASEAN Community (2009–15), para. 4.
[179] Ibid., para. 3.

1.3 THE ASEAN CHARTER AND BEYOND

offices, conciliation and mediation in the settlement of disputes. Article 23(2) of the Charter explicitly states that the parties to a dispute may request the Secretary-General to provide good offices, etc. However, the Charter does not expressly prohibit the Secretary-General from taking the initiative to offer his services where there is a dispute. Nonetheless, a comparison with the equivalent provision in the Vientiane Protocol (which predates the Charter) is instructive. The Vientiane Protocol allows the Secretary-General to volunteer his services to the disputants without waiting to be asked.[180]

The role of the Secretary-General has evolved from just administering the organisation. He is expected to engage with external parties as the face of ASEAN, as well as with the ASEAN public to create a people-centred ASEAN community. ASEAN now participates in G20 meetings and receives invitations to cooperate with organisations like the World Bank, OSCE and IMF. However, there is tension between the concept of the Secretary-General as a minister who should be given a greater role in the management of ASEAN's external relations as envisaged by the EPG and a Secretary-General who is merely the Chief Administrative Officer of ASEAN. It is vital that the member states decide exactly what role they expect the Secretary-General to play in the creation of the ASEAN community – is he just to be a glorified secretary or something more significant? During the term of the previous incumbent, Dr Surin Pitsuwan of Thailand, it appeared that the member states were concerned to keep the

---

[180] 2004 Protocol on Enhanced Dispute Settlement Mechanism, Article 4.

Secretary-General on a short leash. For instance, under the Protocol to the ASEAN Charter on Dispute Settlement Mechanisms, 2010 disputants must concur on a third arbitrator, failing which the appointment will be made by the Chair of the ACC on the recommendation of the Secretary-General. The Secretary-General, however, has to consult the Committee of Permanent Representatives before making his recommendation.[181] Considering that the Permanent Representatives rank as ambassadors while the Secretary-General has ministerial status, this is incongruous to say the least.

It was recognised that ASEC needed a body of dedicated professional staff to meet the new challenges. Two new Deputy Secretaries-General were to be added.[182] The logic of professionalisation of ASEC would have pointed to open recruitment of the new Deputy Secretaries-General. Unfortunately, in a retrograde step, the HLTF decided that only two of the four DSGs would be openly recruited. The other two would be appointed by member states in alphabetical rotation, just as the Secretary-General.[183] This was to assuage the concerns of some of the member states that their nationals would not have a chance to occupy the DSG posts if these were to be filled entirely by open recruitment. The net effect, however, is to limit the professional effectiveness of ASEC, since there is no open competition for the posts. Further diluting the professionalism of ASEC, the other two openly

---

[181] Protocol to the ASEAN Charter on Dispute Settlement Mechanisms 2010, rule 1(4)(b) of Annex 4.
[182] Report of the Eminent Persons' Group on the ASEAN Charter, para. 37.
[183] ASEAN Charter, Article 11.

recruited DSGs can only serve for a maximum of two three-year terms,[184] which hardly makes the post attractive as a career option for the talented. The net effect of the HLTF negotiations was to create an apex of the Secretariat comprising nationals of five member states – the Secretary-General and his four deputies, all of whom must come from different countries.[185] Politically, this may be expedient as it ensures that ASEC is not dominated by nationals of a single member state. From the point of view of professionalism, however, the situation is suboptimal. It is not a case of the best man for the job, but rather an exercise in division of the offices amongst the member states so that each has a 'fair' chance of representation at the top. The practical significance is that there will not be a core of experienced ASEAN administrators at the helm, since the game of musical chairs will ensure that no one remains in office too long. Indeed, in 2012 ASEAN lost all four DSGs and the Secretary-General. By the beginning of 2013 a completely new team was in place.

(1.3.2.4) The Committee of Permanent Representatives

The EPG recommended that the member states appoint full-time Permanent Representatives (PRs) to ASEAN, resident in Jakarta, in order to facilitate coordination.[186] The idea for such a committee had in fact been first mooted as early as 1982 in a report of a Task Force for the Strengthening of the ASEAN Secretariat chaired by Mr Anand Panyarachun of

---

[184] Ibid., Article 11(6)(b). [185] Ibid., Article 11(5).
[186] Report of the Eminent Persons' Group on the ASEAN Charter, Executive Summary, para. 7.

Thailand.[187] These PRs would take on the role hitherto played by the ASEAN Standing Committee.[188] The recommendation was easy to make; implementing it was quite a different matter.

According to Article 12(2) of the Charter, the Committee of Permanent Representatives (CPR) is to support the work of the ASEAN Community Councils, facilitate ASEAN cooperation with external parties and 'liaise with the Secretary-General of ASEAN and the ASEAN Secretariat on all subjects relevant to its work'. The problem is that nowhere is it defined exactly what the CPR can or should do to fulfil the tasks conferred upon it.

The Terms of Reference (TOR) for the Committee of Permanent Representatives to ASEAN was approved by the Forty-first ASEAN Ministerial Meeting in July 2008. It was drafted by the PRs themselves, apparently with very little input from trained lawyers. Among the tasks specifically entrusted to the CPR are:

(a) assisting in the preparation of the meetings of the ASEAN Summit;
(b) coordinating the implementation of agreements and decisions of the ASEAN Summit;
(c) acting as the approving authority for ASEAN projects funded from ASEAN central funds;
(d) approving the operational budget of ASEC.

---

[187] See Severino, *Southeast Asia*, p. 23.
[188] In an oversight, the ASEAN Standing Committee is still listed as a sectoral ministerial body under the Political-Security Community in Annex 1 of the Charter.

1.3 THE ASEAN CHARTER AND BEYOND

The CPR also is supposed to assist in considering and coordinating the reports of the Community Councils, the Secretary-General's annual report and the report of the ASEAN Foundation. Paragraph 6 of the TOR gives the CPR power to oversee the operations of the ASEAN Secretariat and related ASEAN institutions. They also 'coordinate' with the Secretary-General in the performance of his role to monitor the implementation of ASEAN decisions and agreements.

In conversation with one of the authors, one PR likened the CPR to the board of directors of a company, with the Secretary-General more in the position of the Chief Operating Officer. This was not a view shared by all the PRs. It appears that the exact relationship between the CPR on the one hand and the Secretary-General and ASEC on the other is not entirely clear even now. Is the Secretary-General subject to the direct supervision and control of the CPR? How far should the CPR go in overseeing the operations of ASEC? The problem is compounded by the fact that the Secretary-General is of ministerial rank while the PRs are only ambassadors. Indeed, the first Secretary-General after the coming into force of the Charter, Dr Surin Pitsuwan, was Foreign Minister of Thailand at one stage and clearly outranked all the PRs. The Secretary-General has identified the tension between the CPR and ASEC as a factor that undermines community building efforts.

At the time of writing, the modus vivendi between ASEC and the CPR has yet to be fully worked out. Some PRs expressed the view that the CPR is spending too much time micro-managing the Secretariat at the expense of more strategic big-picture issues. The CPR also has not been able to play a significant role in coordinating across the Community Councils. Lack of manpower resources is one of the problems. Lack of a clear mandate is another. No doubt these teething problems will work themselves out over the years, but until that happens the efficiency of ASEAN as an organisation will be compromised.

Chapter 2

Towards an ASEAN community

According to the EPG on the ASEAN Charter, the ultimate end point is the creation of an ASEAN Union.[1] What form this is to take was not spelled out, and indeed there has been no official mention of this subsequent to the presentation of the Report of the Eminent Persons' Group.[2] The aim of creating an ASEAN Community remains alive, however. The target date is 2015, as decided at the Twelfth ASEAN Summit in Cebu in January 2007.[3] Whether it is a Union or Community to be formed, clearly much more has to be done to foster the rules-based culture that closer integration requires. There are two essential elements: first, there has to be an effective mechanism for settling disagreements among the member states that goes beyond mere political patching; secondly, there must be a formal system for promulgating, interpreting and enforcing the rules that are necessary for the creation of a cohesive ASEAN Community. Logically, the creation of rules should come first; but in the ASEAN context

---

[1] Report of the Eminent Persons' Group on the ASEAN Charter, para. 23.
[2] When it came to drafting the Charter, no mention was made of an ASEAN Union. This was deliberate. However, the idea has not been formally abandoned by the leaders. Given the history of the ASEAN Charter itself, one can never exclude the possibility of the revival of the Union idea at some indeterminate point in the future.
[3] See the Cebu Declaration on the Acceleration of the Establishment of an ASEAN Community.

there are quite enough rules, the principal problem being enforcement. ASEAN lacks a culture of keeping to the grandiose plans of action, blueprints and roadmaps that each Summit creates. This must change if the ambition to create an ASEAN Community based on the rule of law is to succeed.

To appreciate the need for a proper legal service, it is necessary to examine the current reality as far as rule-making and dispute settlement are concerned. Much of what follows is based on the experience of one of the authors and discussion with diplomats and officials involved in ASEAN activities.

2.1 The current reality

2.1.1 *The making of rules*

A rules-based organisation must have some means for making rules. The current method depends largely, if not exclusively, on the member states themselves. The rules that bind ASEAN member states are to be found in the many treaties, agreements, memoranda of understanding and protocols that are produced after the ASEAN Summits and sectoral meetings in the course of a year. Since the adoption of the ASEAN Charter in November 2007 there have been over sixty such intergovernmental agreements.[4] Some of these are between ASEAN and external parties like China, Japan, Korea, India, Australia and New Zealand, including one plurilateral Agreement establishing the ASEAN–Australia–New Zealand Free Trade

---

[4] Compiled from the Table of Ratifications maintained by the ASEAN Secretariat.

2.1 THE CURRENT REALITY

Area (AANZFTA). The majority are agreements among the ASEAN member states themselves. These are the source of the rules that bind the organisation.

Taking the ASEAN Charter itself as typical, the process starts with a draft put up either by the Secretariat[5] or by the member state delegations. At the beginning of the negotiations for the Charter, it was proposed by a delegation that the task of drafting should be split among the member state delegations for efficiency. This was not agreed to. Instead, the different delegations put up their drafts of various articles. The modus operandi that eventually emerged was that ASEC would put up a draft, which was worked on by the High Level Task Force (HLTF) and then sent for 'scrubbing' by the legal experts. Each delegation had one or more lawyers attached, whose task it was to clean up the language of the text agreed to by the HLTF and work out the ambiguities. Where there was disagreement over the precise formulation, words or phrases would be 'bracketed' by the HLTF, i.e., placed in square brackets for further consideration by the lawyers. It was then up to the experts to close the gaps between the positions of the national delegations. Often, these experts would propose alternative language for the consideration of the HLTF.

The Charter-drafting process is instructive in illustrating the dire need for some professional lawyers at the

[5] In March 2004 Malaysia presented a paper on reform of the institutional framework of ASEAN at the FMM retreat in Ha Long Bay, Vietnam. Subsequently, ASEC prepared a draft Charter. However, this was not used as the basis for the ASEAN Charter. Instead, the draft annexed to the Report of the Eminent Persons' Group was used. This had been prepared by the Indonesian EPG Member, Mr Ali Alatas.

ASEAN level. It was fortunate that the incumbent Secretary-General, Mr Ong Keng Yong, was a trained lawyer. However, he had no legal counsel at his side to assist. Nor did the HLTF have the benefit of a neutral legal adviser who could help to bridge the gaps between the national positions in a non-partisan fashion. It was fortunate that members of the HLTF got along well and were competently shepherded along by the Chairman. One cannot count on this happy state of affairs in every ASEAN meeting.

English was not the first language of most of the members of the HLTF. This did not deter some from quibbling over the nuances of English terms. Matters were made more difficult since only a small minority of the members of the HLTF were lawyers. Even fewer were international lawyers. The document that finally emerged was a compromise, inelegantly drafted and more wordy than necessary. This was inevitable given the fact that there was no neutral third party to whom the process of drafting could be entrusted. National positions naturally intruded often. In one particularly sensitive instance, Article 14 on the ASEAN Human Rights Body, the disagreements were so fierce that negotiations almost broke down, some delegations threatening to walk away. The formulation that was finally agreed was so finely balanced that when the HLTF sent it to the Foreign Ministers for approval, it was with a plea not to change any of the words. The Foreign Ministers did change the wording, but since they were the final arbiters of the issue the controversy was disposed of by their decision.

The role of the lawyers should be noted. Even after the Charter was adopted, there were many areas where details

2.1 THE CURRENT REALITY

had to be filled in. In a domestic context, the Charter can be likened to primary legislation while the details – regulations, rules of procedure, etc. – are secondary legislation. The secondary legislation in the case of the Charter consisted of a protocol on the dispute settlement mechanism, an agreement on the privileges and immunities of ASEAN and, most difficult of all, the terms of reference of the Human Rights Body (subsequently named the ASEAN Intergovernmental Commission on Human Rights). The first two were entrusted to another High Level Legal Experts' Group,[6] while the last was negotiated by senior officials.[7] Lawyers play a secondary role where the agreements are not legal in nature. It will be appreciated from the foregoing that the process of drafting ASEAN rules is extremely ad hoc in nature.

There is at present no system for preparing drafts for ASEAN meetings. That task is left to the Chair. A member state that has a particular interest in a matter may also circulate a draft for discussion. It does not help that all the agreements are in English. This is declared to be the working language of ASEAN.[8] There was no controversy about this during the negotiations for the ASEAN Charter, since no other language commonly used in ASEAN would have been comprehensible in all ten member states. Unfortunately, English is an official language only in the Philippines and Singapore.

---

[6] See the Joint Communiqué of the Forty-first AMM, para. 11.
[7] A High Level Panel on the ASEAN Human Rights Body was set up by the Forty-first ASEAN Ministerial Meeting (July 2008). See the Joint Communiqué of the Forty-first AMM, para. 10.
[8] Article 34.

It is commonly understood in Malaysia and Brunei because of the colonial link. English language competency in Myanmar appears to have deteriorated considerably, despite that same colonial link. As for Vietnam, Laos and Cambodia, the language spoken by the older generation was French. The Indonesians do not retain much attachment to Dutch, while the Thais were never colonised. The effect of this varied history is that many of the national delegations struggle with the English language during ASEAN meetings. This is a particular problem for the CLMV,[9] where officials with English-language competence are rare. Even in a grouping like the ASEAN Senior Legal Officials' Meeting (ASLOM) discussion is constrained by the limited English of many of the members of the CLMV delegations, as well as Thailand and Indonesia. ASEC cannot and does not staff all of the myriad officials' and sectoral ministers' meetings, which are left very much to their own devices when it comes to the drafting of documents. Nor is it in a position to provide interpreters, that being left to the national delegations. Indeed, the Charter-drafting process was atypical in that the draft was put up by ASEC on the basis of the Report of the Eminent Persons' Group.

One can imagine the problems that arise when non-English speakers try to draft legal documents in the English language. Even in an English-speaking country this is a specialist skill (though professional lawyers can be equally guilty of perpetrating linguistic atrocities). The deficiencies of the current ad hoc process are apparent when one examines the

---

[9] A handy acronym for the new ASEAN members, viz., Cambodia, Laos, Myanmar and Vietnam.

2.1 THE CURRENT REALITY

'subsidiary legislation' that fills in the blanks of the ASEAN Charter. Legal drafting in English is hard enough when done by trained legislative draughtsmen; when attempted by non-lawyers whose first language is not English, the end product is unlikely to be a model of either logic or clarity.

2.1.2 *The settlement of disputes*

The original 1967 Bangkok Declaration that founded ASEAN made no provision for institutions of any sort beyond a regular meeting of the Foreign Ministers. In 1971 ASEAN issued the ZOPFAN Declaration,[10] which was 'inspired by the worthy aims and objectives of the United Nations, in particular by the principles of respect for the sovereignty and territorial integrity of all states, abstention from threat or use of force, peaceful settlement of international disputes, equal rights and self-determination and non-interference in affairs of States', according to its Preamble. This represented the first explicit reference to peaceful settlement of international disputes among ASEAN countries. There was no mechanism set up to achieve this aim. Troubles within the ASEAN family were settled by diplomacy or quietly allowed to fade into the background.[11] This was how ASEAN functioned for four decades. The ASEAN Charter was designed

---

[10] The Zone of Peace, Freedom and Neutrality Declaration (November 1971).
[11] For instance, the dispute between Malaysia and the Philippines over Sabah which had led to a rupture of diplomatic relations between the two countries in 1963 remains unresolved even today. The Philippines has not yet formally dropped its claim to Sabah. See Severino, *Southeast Asia*, pp. 164–6.

to change this unsatisfactory situation and create the legal framework for ASEAN as a rules-based organisation.

The settlement of disputes is dealt with in Chapter VIII of the Charter. To recapitulate: disputes which do not concern the interpretation or application of any ASEAN instrument are to be resolved in accordance with the Treaty of Amity and Cooperation in Southeast Asia (TAC).[12] Economic disputes will be settled by recourse to the ASEAN Protocol on Enhanced Dispute Settlement Mechanism (the Vientiane Protocol).[13] As for other sorts of disputes, it is specifically stated in Article 22(2) that dispute settlement mechanisms must be established in all fields of ASEAN cooperation. In pursuance of this, a High Level Experts Group (HLEG) was set up and tasked with fleshing out the dispute settlement mechanism.[14] The HLEG's recommendations resulted in the Protocol to the ASEAN Charter on Dispute Settlement Mechanisms (the DSM Protocol), signed by the Foreign Ministers of the ASEAN states on 8 April 2010 in Hanoi.[15] The DSM Protocol is meant to fill the gaps where the TAC and Vientiane Protocol do not apply.

(2.1.2.1) The Treaty of Amity and Cooperation

The 1976 Declaration of ASEAN Concord (Bali Concord)[16] declared that 'Member states, in the spirit of ASEAN solidarity, shall rely exclusively on peaceful processes in the

---

[12] ASEAN Charter, Article 24(2).   [13] Ibid., Article 24(3).
[14] See the Joint Communiqué of the Forty-first AMM, para. 11.
[15] Though not yet in effect. See the Table of Ratifications maintained by the ASEAN Secretariat on its website (www.asean.org).
[16] Adopted at the First ASEAN Summit in Bali, Indonesia, in February 1976.

2.1 THE CURRENT REALITY

settlement of intra-regional differences.' The member states renounced the use of force and committed themselves to settlement of differences or disputes by peaceful means in Article 2 of the Treaty of Amity and Cooperation in Southeast Asia (TAC).[17] Chapter IV of the TAC covers the Pacific Settlement of Disputes. The ASEAN Charter now provides that disputes that do not concern the 'interpretation or application of any ASEAN instrument' shall be resolved in accordance with the TAC.[18]

Article 10 of the TAC states that 'Each High Contracting Party shall not in any manner or form participate in any activity which shall constitute a threat to the political and economic stability, sovereignty, or territorial integrity of another High Contracting Party.' Article 13 obliges the High Contracting Parties to refrain from the threat or use of force and settle disputes among themselves through friendly negotiations. The dispute settlement mechanism under the TAC consists of a High Council comprising one representative at ministerial level from each of the ten ASEAN member states together with representatives of non-ASEAN states which are directly involved in the dispute.[19] This High Council is

---

[17] Signed by the leaders of the five original ASEAN member states on the same date as the Bali Concord.

[18] ASEAN Charter, Article 24(2). Strictly speaking, the TAC only applies to disputes that are likely to disturb regional peace and harmony. The mechanism created by the TAC is probably too cumbersome to be invoked for other sorts of disputes.

[19] Treaty of Amity and Cooperation in Southeast Asia, Article 14 (as amended by the First Protocol, signed in Manila on 15 December 1987) and Rule 3 of the Rules of Procedure (adopted on 23 July 2001 in Hanoi).

supposed to take cognisance of any 'disputes or situations likely to disturb regional peace and harmony'.[20] If negotiations do not succeed in settling the dispute, the High Council's role is to recommend 'appropriate means of settlement such as good offices, mediation, inquiry or conciliation'.[21] The High Council itself may offer its good offices. If the parties agree the High Council may constitute itself as a committee of mediation, inquiry or conciliation.[22]

There are three glaring weaknesses in the scheme set up in Chapter IV of the TAC. First, and most significant, Articles 14 and 15 do not apply unless the parties to the dispute agree. Any of the disputants can block the use of the dispute settlement mechanism. The non-mandatory nature of the procedure means that it will be used only if there is a significant change in the political mindset of the High Contracting Parties in favour of objective dispute settlement. As things stand, the solution to any dispute threatening to disturb peace and harmony in the region will be political.

The second weakness as far as ASEAN member states are concerned is that the TAC procedure allows countries other than ASEAN member states to get involved in the dispute settlement process. At the Third ASEAN Summit held in Manila in 1987 the TAC was amended to allow for the accession of states outside Southeast Asia. Under rule 14 of the Rules of Procedure non-ASEAN member states may be represented as observers at meetings of the High Council. This means that these non-ASEAN states will be able to watch

---

[20] Treaty of Amity and Cooperation in Southeast Asia, Article 14.
[21] Ibid., Article 15.   [22] Ibid.

2.1 THE CURRENT REALITY

and (with the permission of the High Council) speak at meetings. Washing of dirty linen in public is bad enough; washing it in full view of people outside the family is worse. There is a view among some ASEAN members, ventilated during the negotiations on the ASEAN Charter, that 'outsiders' should not be part of any dispute settlement mechanism. This is probably the underlying motive for the amendment of the TAC in 2010 to provide that a non-ASEAN High Contracting Party will not form part of the High Council unless that party is directly involved in a dispute to which the TAC applies.[23] Regional solutions for regional problems is the mantra. Although this view does not command the unanimous agreement of all the ASEAN member states, it nonetheless remains strongly held in some quarters. In the light of the history of Southeast Asia, the wariness about interference by outside powers is entirely understandable.

The third weakness is that there is no explicit provision for arbitration or adjudication by a court or tribunal. Good offices, mediation, inquiry and conciliation are essentially non-legal modes of dispute settlement. They supplement direct political negotiations. This reluctance to submit to binding dispute settlement has characterised the 'ASEAN way' from the very start. Any dispute settlement under the TAC will have to be consensual rather than confrontational. More importantly, there will not be a public loss of face. This approach accords with the primary role of ASEAN as a mechanism to foster trust among the member states.

---

[23] Third Protocol Amending the Treaty of Amity and Cooperation in Southeast Asia, Article 2. In force 12 June 2012.

One suspects that this is driven by realpolitik. International courts and arbitrators cannot be controlled by governments. In countries where the rule of law is weak, it is perhaps too much to expect that a government would willingly cede the power to decide an international political dispute to neutral outside parties. Nonetheless, neutral dispute settlement is vital if ASEAN is to progress towards a rules-based community. The question is whether there is sufficient political will to do so within the time frame agreed.

The drafters of the TAC clearly recognised the limitations of the dispute settlement mechanism that they had created. In Article 17 it is specifically provided that nothing in the TAC shall preclude recourse to the modes of settlement in Article 33(1) of the UN Charter, though the High Contracting parties are 'encouraged' to solve disputes by 'friendly negotiations' before resorting to such other modes of dispute settlement. This provision is mirrored in Article 28 of the ASEAN Charter.

The TAC might have been invoked in the dispute between Malaysia and Indonesia over the islands of Sipadan and Ligitan. Indonesia wanted to bring the Ligitan/Sipadan dispute to the High Council but Malaysia refused, fearing that other ASEAN members would be partial to Indonesia.[24] In the end the dispute was referred to the International Court of Justice (ICJ) instead.[25] Interestingly, the Special Agreement

---

[24] See Severino, *Southeast Asia*, pp. 12–13.
[25] President Soeharto decided to submit the matter to the ICJ despite the objections of his officials. Indonesia lost the case. See *Case Concerning Sovereignty over Pulau Ligitan and Pulau Sipadan* (Judgment 17 December 2002).

2.1 THE CURRENT REALITY

for submission of the case to the ICJ stated in the preamble that the parties desired 'that this dispute should be settled in the spirit of friendly relations existing between the Parties as enunciated in the 1976 Treaty of Amity and Cooperation in Southeast Asia'.[26]

A more recent occasion for possible invocation of the TAC was the dispute between Thailand and Cambodia over the area surrounding the Temple of Preah Vihear (discussed in more detail below). In July 2008 Singapore held the Chairmanship of ASEAN. The Foreign Ministers met informally in Singapore to discuss the issue. The possibility of using the TAC was raised but not accepted by the parties. Without the cooperation of the disputing parties, ASEAN could do nothing further.

The TAC mechanism is not likely to be used to settle disputes between ASEAN member states. The process is too public, involving the convening of a High Council at which non-ASEAN High Contracting Parties may be represented as observers. Rather, the TAC is likely be used as an inspirational document, committing the High Contracting Parties to peaceful settlement of their disputes, as happened in the Ligitan/Sipadan case between Indonesia and Malaysia. If a legally binding result is desired, the TAC does allow other international dispute settlement mechanisms to be invoked.

---

[26] The Special Agreement was signed on 31 May 1997 by Mr Ali Alatas, Foreign Minister of Indonesia and Datuk Abdullah Ahmad Badawi, Foreign Minister of Malaysia. Mr Alatas was a member of the EPG that conceptualised the Charter. Datuk Abdullah Badawi was Prime Minister of Malaysia when the Charter was presented to the Thirteenth ASEAN Summit in Singapore.

This might even mean recourse to the ICJ, as in the Sipadan/Ligitan case. It is also possible that the TAC route will lead indirectly to the arbitration procedure now provided in the 2010 Protocol to the ASEAN Charter on Dispute Settlement Mechanisms (discussed below).

(2.1.2.2) Economic disputes

Economic integration is now the cornerstone of ASEAN community. Of the three pillars, this is the most advanced. The creation of an ASEAN Economic Community cannot take place without the existence of some means of settling disagreements amongst the member states over interpretation and implementation of the various economic agreements. The creation of such a dispute settlement mechanism was an early priority of ASEAN.

Article 9 of the 1992 Framework Agreement on Enhancing ASEAN Economic Cooperation provided for the establishment of a dispute settlement mechanism, but it took four more years before the ASEAN states signed the Manila Protocol on Dispute Settlement Mechanism. The Manila Protocol was superseded in 2004 by the Protocol on Enhanced Dispute Settlement Mechanism, signed in Vientiane by the Economic Ministers at the Eleventh ASEAN Summit (the Vientiane Protocol).

The Vientiane Protocol is administered by the Senior Economic Officials' Meeting (SEOM). It applies to disputes arising under the 1992 Framework Agreement on Enhancing ASEAN Economic Cooperation or other economic agreements set out in Appendix I to the Protocol, as well as future ASEAN economic agreements (referred to as 'covered agreements').

2.1 THE CURRENT REALITY

The ASEAN Charter extended the coverage of the Vientiane Protocol to all ASEAN economic agreements.[27] Article 4 of the Protocol provides for good offices, conciliation or mediation. It is specifically provided that the Secretary-General of ASEAN may offer good offices, conciliation or mediation with a view to assisting in the settlement of a dispute, giving him a potentially significant role in resolution of such disputes. The High Level Task Force on ASEAN Economic Integration recommended the creation of an ASEAN Compliance Monitoring Body (ACMB) modelled on the Textile Monitoring Body of the World Trade Organization (WTO).[28] This provides an informal non-binding means of resolving disputes. A request may be made for ACMB members from states not involved in the dispute to review the case and make findings within a stipulated time frame. If a finding of non-compliance is made, the guilty state should correct the situation; otherwise the matter has to go to formal dispute settlement.

The core of the dispute settlement mechanism is the mandatory procedure prescribed by the Vientiane Protocol. If there is any dispute under the covered agreements, the aggrieved party will request consultations.[29] The other party must reply within ten days and enter into consultations within thirty days. If it fails to do so, the complainant

---

[27] ASEAN Charter, Article 24(3). This applies 'where not otherwise specifically provided'. It is possible to exclude the operation of the Vientiane Protocol; see e.g., the 2012 ASEAN Agreement on the Movement of Natural Persons, Article 11(2).
[28] This report was annexed to Bali Concord II, adopted at the Ninth ASEAN Summit (October 2003).
[29] 2004 Protocol on Enhanced Dispute Settlement Mechanism, Article 3.

may raise the matter with SEOM.[30] Similarly, the matter may go to SEOM if consultations do not result in a satisfactory resolution of the problem within sixty days.

Once the dispute is raised with SEOM, a panel will be established unless SEOM decides by consensus not to do so.[31] This means in practice that all the members of SEOM must either agree not to do so or acquiesce in that decision. SEOM has forty-five days to decide. The decision will be taken either at a SEOM meeting or by circulation. It is specifically provided that non-reply by any member is taken as agreement to the establishment of a panel. This is to avoid the well-known tactic of keeping silent and hoping that the problem will go away. Thus, the default position is that a panel will be established.

The panel's function is to make a report to SEOM,[32] having objectively considered the facts and provisions of the relevant agreements.[33] The panel is obliged to submit its report and recommendations within sixty days.[34] SEOM must adopt the report within thirty days unless there is a consensus not to do so or a party notifies its decision to appeal.[35] If the decision to adopt is not made at a formal meeting, it will be done by circulation and a non-reply is again treated as agreement to adopt.

Appeals go to an appellate body established by the ASEAN Economic Ministers' Meeting.[36] An appeal must be

---

[30] Ibid., Article 5(1). [31] Ibid. [32] Ibid., Article 6(1).
[33] Ibid., Article 7.
[34] Ibid., Article 8(2). Exceptionally, it may take a further ten days if necessary.
[35] Ibid., Article 9(1). [36] Ibid., Article 12.

2.1 THE CURRENT REALITY

concluded within sixty days.[37] Appeals are limited to issues of law and interpretation. The Appellate Body's report shall be adopted by SEOM within thirty days unless there is a consensus not to do so.[38] The disputing parties are obliged to accept the report unconditionally[39] and comply within sixty days of the report of the panel or Appellate Body, as the case may be.[40] SEOM is to oversee compliance.[41] Non-compliance attracts sanctions under the Protocol. Compensation may be paid by the offending party. Article 16(2) sets out a time frame within which negotiations for compensation must be entered into. If no satisfactory compensation has been agreed within the stipulated period, the aggrieved party may request authorisation from SEOM to suspend concessions or other obligations under the covered agreements.[42] SEOM is obliged to grant such authorisation unless there is a consensus to reject the request.[43] Compensation and suspension of concessions are temporary measures. The offending state is obliged to comply with its obligations under the covered agreements.[44] If the offending party continues to be recalcitrant, the matter may be referred to the ASEAN Summit for a decision under Article 27(2) of the ASEAN Charter.

The Vientiane Protocol has clear similarities to the dispute settlement procedure of the WTO,[45] especially with its

---

[37] Ibid., Article 12(5); exceptionally, the Appellate Body may take longer, but the maximum is ninety days.
[38] Ibid., Article 12(13).   [39] Ibid.   [40] Ibid., Article 15(1).
[41] Ibid., Article 15(6).   [42] Ibid., Article 16(2).   [43] Ibid., Article 16(6).
[44] Ibid., Articles 16(1) and 16(9).
[45] See the WTO's Understanding on Rules and Procedures Governing the Settlement of Disputes.

strict timelines and provisions to ensure that the panel and appellate reports are adopted unless there is a consensus against it. Such a mechanism is vital if the ASEAN Free Trade Area is to function properly. It has never been invoked, so no assessment of its effectiveness can be made.[46] However, the WTO Dispute Settlement Mechanism has been invoked by Singapore against Malaysia,[47] Singapore against the Philippines and the Philippines against Thailand.[48] The Singapore case against Malaysia was withdrawn after the underlying cause of complaint was addressed. The second Singapore case against the Philippines was settled amicably after consultations between then-Minister of Trade and Industry George Yeo and his Filipino counterpart Mar Roxas. The two had excellent relations, which allowed the matter to be resolved without convening a panel. The Philippines paid some compensation. The Philippine case against Thailand is the only one to have proceeded to adjudication.

The Philippines requested consultations with Thailand on 7 February 2008. A panel was established and duly presented its final report, finding in favour of

[46] At least one commentator has criticised the timelines as unrealistic: see Vergano, 'The ASEAN Dispute Settlement Mechanism and its Role in a Rules-Based Community: Overview and Critical Comparison', Asian International Economic Law Network (AIELN) Inaugural Conference, 30 June 2009, available at aielni.web.fc2.com/ Vergano_panel4.pdf. Scepticism as to the effectiveness of the system has been expressed to one of the authors by some diplomats based in Jakarta.
[47] Dispute DS1, 1995.
[48] Dispute DS371, 2008. The panel report recommending that Thailand bring the offending measures into conformity with its obligations was adopted on 15 July 2011.

2.1 THE CURRENT REALITY

the Philippines. Thailand appealed and lost. The Appellate Body's report was adopted on 15 July 2011. On 11 August 2011 Thailand informed the Dispute Settlement Body that it intended to implement the recommendations and rulings 'in a manner that respects its WTO obligations'. Thailand was given a reasonable time to do this after negotiations with the Philippines. The sharp contrast with the Preah Vihear case should be noted. This matter arose at almost exactly the same time as the Preah Vihear problem. The WTO proceedings did not provoke the kind of reaction that Preah Vihear elicited in Thailand. One infers that this was because the issue did not become politicised by contending factions in Thailand.

The Philippines/Thailand dispute could have been resolved in accordance with the Vientiane Protocol.[49] It was not. In conversation with one of the authors a senior ASEAN official expressed the view that member states are still not confident of the effectiveness of the ASEAN dispute settlement mechanism. If this is true, it is a bad portent for the creation of a rules-based ASEAN Economic Community by the declared deadline. One can only speculate as to the exact nature of the reservations on the part of the Philippines, which was the complainant state. From the point of view of the Ministry of Foreign Affairs of any ASEAN state, invoking a binding dispute settlement mechanism is a serious step. When given the choice between a tested mechanism and an untested one, caution dictates that the tested mechanism

---

[49] See Dispute DS371. The Philippines had requested consultations with Thailand on 7 February 2008. The Vientiane Protocol came into force on 29 November 2004.

should be chosen. This leads to a policy dilemma: if no member state chooses to use the Vientiane Protocol, it will never be tested; but if the Protocol is invoked and something goes wrong, there will be recriminations. No one wants to be first into uncharted waters. Therefore, a policy decision has to be made at the highest level to prefer the ASEAN route to the WTO one. If ASEAN member states are serious about creating an economic community by 2015, they need to take the Vientiane Protocol seriously when disagreements arise.

(2.1.2.3) Non-economic disputes

The Protocol to the ASEAN Charter on Dispute Settlement Mechanisms (the DSM Protocol)[50] covers other disputes that do not fall within the ambit of the TAC or the Vientiane Protocol.

The parties to a dispute may agree to resort to good offices, conciliation or mediation.[51] The DSM Protocol provides detailed rules of procedure for this in Annexes 1–3. Note the rather strict and artificial distinction between mediation and conciliation. The role of the mediator is to 'help facilitate communication and negotiation between the parties'.[52] A conciliator, in contrast, may make proposals for settlement of the dispute.[53] In practice, mediation often blends into

---

[50] This was signed by the Foreign Ministers of the ASEAN states on 8 April 2010 in Hanoi but is not yet in effect. See the Table of Ratifications maintained by the ASEAN Secretariat on its website (www.asean.org).
[51] ASEAN Charter, Article 23(1).
[52] Annex 2 to the DSM Protocol, rule 2.
[53] Annex 3 to the DSM Protocol, rule 3(3).

2.1 THE CURRENT REALITY

conciliation in a seamless manner.[54] It would be unwise to keep the two modes as distinct as the DSM Protocol envisages. The aim of good offices, conciliation or mediation is to achieve an amicable settlement of the dispute, viz., one under which neither party loses face. Given the consensual nature of ASEAN relations, this is likely to be the preferred mode of dispute settlement.

The parties may also request the Chairman of ASEAN or the Secretary-General to provide such good offices, conciliation and mediation.[55] Note the similarity to the scheme under the TAC and the Vientiane Protocol. Unlike under the Vientiane Protocol, however, the Secretary-General is not to take the initiative to offer assistance. This is deliberate. There appeared to be a concern on the part of some HLTF delegations that an activist Secretary-General would butt in without being invited. However, the Charter does not prohibit the Secretary-General volunteering his good offices, etc. Nor does the Charter state that all the parties to the dispute must concur in requesting good offices, etc.[56] It would accord with the spirit of the Charter (which provides that disputes should be resolved peacefully in a timely

---

[54] For example, in 2011 Indonesian Foreign Minister Marty Natalegawa mediated the dispute between Cambodia and Thailand over the Temple of Preah Vihear. Not only did he shuttle between the parties, he also brokered a ceasefire and suggested the insertion of Indonesian observers. This is discussed in more detail below.

[55] ASEAN Charter, Article 23(2).

[56] In reality, though, it is unlikely that the Secretary-General will make any headway unless the parties are willing to accept his assistance.

manner)[57] as well as the recommendations of the EPG if any party could make such a request, even in the absence of agreement by the other party. Otherwise, an intransigent party could block settlement of the dispute indefinitely. This would hardly conduce to creating a community based on the rule of law, which is one of the primary aims of the Charter.[58] The involvement of the Chairman of ASEAN in dispute settlement gives a greater significance to the role of the ASEAN Chair, which rotates among the member states in alphabetical order. The effectiveness of the Chair depends largely on the personality of the Foreign Minister and head of government of the country that holds it; effectiveness is not a function of size alone.

However, it would be unwise to have a dispute settlement mechanism based entirely on consensual mechanisms. When trouble broke out between Cambodia and Thailand in 2003 over alleged remarks by a Thai actress regarding ownership of Angkor Wat, the incumbent Secretary-General Ong Keng Yong offered ASEAN's assistance in resolving matters; he was rebuffed by Cambodia.[59] In 2008 a dispute flared up between Cambodia and Thailand over the Temple of Preah Vihear. Singaporean Foreign Minister George Yeo, who occupied the Chair at that time, hosted an informal gathering of ASEAN Foreign Ministers at the Botanic Gardens in Singapore. At first the Thai Foreign Minister declined to attend.

[57] ASEAN Charter, Article 22(1).
[58] Ibid., Preamble and Articles 1(7), 2(2)(h), 2(2)(n).
[59] Severino, *Southeast Asia*, pp. 14–15. Confirmed to one of the authors by Mr Ong himself.

2.1 THE CURRENT REALITY

However, Foreign Minister Yeo managed to persuade him to go to Singapore. The ASEAN Foreign Ministers offered the 'facilities of ASEAN' to mediate the dispute, recognising the importance of maintaining peace and stability of the region.[60] A proposal was made for the formation of an ASEAN Contact Group to help support the efforts of the disputing parties to find a peaceful solution.[61] There was no consensus among the group, however, neither Cambodia nor Thailand being willing at that point to have ASEAN involved. Subsequently, in 2010, Cambodian Foreign Minister Hor Namhong wrote to Vietnamese Foreign Minister Pham Gia Khiem in his capacity as ASEAN Chair requesting mediation of the dispute under the Charter.[62] This time Thailand again declined to let the ASEAN Chair mediate.[63] Clearly something more robust is required if disputes between member states are to be settled by legally binding means.

Article 25 of the Charter is the key provision. During the Charter-drafting process there was some hard bargaining before agreement was reached on this. A serious difference of opinion emerged over the wording of Article 25. An initial proposal to require the establishment of appropriate dispute settlement mechanisms 'including adjudication' ran into resistance. It was apparent during the negotiations that some

---

[60] See Statement by Singaporean Minister for Foreign Affairs George Yeo, 22 July 2008. Available on the website of the Singapore Ministry of Foreign Affairs: www.mfa.gov.sg.
[61] Ibid.
[62] International Crisis Group Asia Report No. 215, 'Waging Peace: ASEAN and the Thai–Cambodian Border Conflict' (6 December 2011), n. 105.
[63] Ibid., p. 15.

member states preferred less-formal means of dispute settlement. The feeling was that there should be non-legal avenues for dispute settlement rather than a formal process. This view did not commend itself to the majority of the HLTF members. It was felt that any dispute settlement mechanism that did not allow for a legally binding settlement of disputes could not be taken seriously. The compromise reached is encapsulated in Article 25, which provides that 'appropriate dispute settlement mechanisms, *including arbitration*, shall be established for disputes which concern the interpretation or application of this Charter and other ASEAN instruments' (emphasis added).

Arbitration is now provided for in Articles 10–17 and Annex 4 of the DSM Protocol. The first step is a request for consultations. The DSM Protocol provides that a complainant may request consultations, which must be completed within ninety days unless the parties otherwise agree.[64] If the respondent does not agree to enter into consultations or the consultations do not result in a settlement of the dispute, the complainant may request the appointment of an arbitral tribunal.[65] If the respondent does not agree to the appointment of an arbitral tribunal, the matter will be referred to the ASEAN Coordinating Council (ACC),[66] which comprises the Foreign Ministers of the ASEAN members.[67] The ACC can direct the parties to settle the dispute by good offices,

---

[64] Protocol to the ASEAN Charter on Dispute Settlement Mechanisms 2010, Article 5.
[65] Ibid., Article 8(1).   [66] Ibid., Article 8(4).
[67] ASEAN Charter, Article 8(1).

2.1 THE CURRENT REALITY

conciliation, mediation or arbitration.[68] The ACC has a maximum of seventy-five days to do this.[69] If the ACC cannot come to a decision, the matter will be referred to the Summit as an unresolved dispute.[70] Contrast this to the 'negative consensus' system under the Vientiane Protocol. Under that Protocol a panel will be established unless there is a consensus not to do so; in other words, the respondent cannot block the establishment of a panel. Under the DSM Protocol there must be a consensus to refer the matter to arbitration. It will be realised that an intransigent party can insist on a political solution by preventing the ACC from coming to a consensus. There will of course be a political price to be paid for this.

Generally, an arbitral tribunal will consist of three arbitrators.[71] Arbitrators are to be chosen from a list maintained by the Secretary-General, each member state being entitled to nominate ten persons.[72] Crucially, arbitrators must

---

[68] Protocol to the ASEAN Charter on Dispute Settlement Mechanisms 2010, Article 9(1).
[69] Ibid., Articles 9(2) and 9(3).
[70] Ibid., Article 9(4). Rules for Reference of Unresolved Disputes to the ASEAN Summit were incorporated as Annex 5 to the DSM Protocol on 27 October 2010.
[71] Rule 1(1) of Annex 4 to the DSM Protocol. Where more than one member state is involved in the dispute, there may be more arbitrators subject to agreement among the parties: Rule 6(1) to Annex 4 of the DSM Protocol.
[72] Rule 5 of Annex 4 to the DSM Protocol. Some members may have capacity problems in populating the list. It is not expressly provided that member states can only nominate their nationals, so it is always open to them to appoint eminent jurists who are not their nationals, though one expects that this will be rare.

be independent of the parties and not take instructions from them.[73] Each party appoints one arbitrator. They must concur on the third arbitrator, failing which the appointment will be made by the Chair of the ACC on the recommendation of the Secretary-General (who has to consult the Committee of Permanent Representatives).[74] Significantly, Article 11(3) implicitly recognises that arbitrators can come from outside ASEAN, since it is stated that the Chair of the arbitral panel shall 'preferably' be a national of an ASEAN state. However, this will happen only in exceptional circumstances.[75] This is another example of the desire to keep matters within the family when it comes to dispute settlement.

As a mechanism to produce a legally binding settlement, the DSM Protocol is set up to fail. It is more a means of fostering a political solution to problems than a proper mode of dispute settlement. This is a consequence of second thoughts by the foreign ministries after the adoption of the ASEAN Charter. As previously explained, some ASEAN member states were reluctant to have a system of compulsory dispute settlement. Having conceded the point during the negotiations on the Charter, they got their way when the DSM Protocol was drafted.

A dispute will only go to arbitration if there is a positive decision on the part of the ACC to allow it. Since

---

[73] Protocol to the ASEAN Charter on Dispute Settlement Mechanisms 2010, Article 11(2)(c).
[74] Rule 1(4)(b) of Annex 4 to the DSM Protocol. Note the implicit desire to circumscribe the freedom of action of the Secretary-General.
[75] Ibid.

2.1 THE CURRENT REALITY

ASEAN works on consensus[76] this will only happen if all the members agree (or can be induced by peer pressure to acquiesce). Thus, it is likely that disputes will continue to be settled by political means, the DSM Protocol notwithstanding. The Protocol has not even been ratified by a single ASEAN member state at the time of writing. The willingness of the member states to do so is a litmus test of the true depth of their commitment to creating a rules-based organisation.

(2.1.2.4) Non-compliance with the result of a dispute settlement mechanism

If there is non-compliance with an arbitral award or the result of any other dispute settlement mechanism, an aggrieved party may refer the matter to the Summit.[77] The notification is to be done through the ASEAN Coordinating Council,[78] at least where the matter concerns an arbitral award or settlement agreement under the DSM Protocol. Nothing is expressly provided in the DSM Protocol regarding non-compliance with awards under the Vientiane Protocol or settlements pursuant to the Treaty of Amity and Cooperation. One expects that a similar procedure will be followed in such cases despite the absence of explicit rules. The ACC is to

---

[76] ASEAN Charter, Article 20(1).   [77] Ibid., Article 27(2).
[78] Rule 1(a) of the Rules for Reference of Non-Compliance to the ASEAN Summit. These rules have been incorporated as Annex 6 to the DSM Protocol as of 2 April 2012. There are also Rules for Reference of Unresolved Disputes to the ASEAN Summit, which were incorporated as Annex 5 to the DSM Protocol on 27 October 2010. Confusingly, rule 2(1) of Annex 5 characterises non-compliance with the instructions of the ACC as an unresolved dispute.

facilitate consultations among the parties to settle the matter without having to involve the Summit.[79] If the problem cannot be resolved, the matter must be referred to the Summit within ninety days or such longer period as the parties to the dispute may agree.[80] The ACC will annex a report with its recommendations when the matter is referred to the Summit.

Once the matter goes to the ASEAN Summit, the resolution of the dispute will not be entirely on the basis of the law. Inevitably, the recommendations of the ACC will be political and not legal in nature. However, there is nothing to prevent the Summit from establishing a legal panel of some sort to assist the leaders in deciding what to do if there is an unresolved dispute or non-compliance with the decision of a dispute settlement body. If ASEAN is serious about becoming a rules-based organisation, it would be far better that some independent legal body advise the leaders instead of having them decide on the basis of the political recommendations of the ACC. It would be immensely damaging to ASEAN's credibility if the result of an arbitration could be overturned or modified on political grounds. Trust in institutions is vital if ASEAN is to fulfil its declared ambitions. That trust can only be fostered if the member states respect the decisions of the dispute settlement mechanisms they have agreed to establish.

---

[79] Rule 3 of the Rules for Reference of Non-Compliance to the ASEAN Summit.

[80] Rule 5(a) of the Rules for Reference of Non-Compliance to the ASEAN Summit.

2.1 THE CURRENT REALITY

2.1.3 Dispute settlement in practice

(2.1.3.1) The Preah Vihear case[81]

Cambodia was not one of the original five ASEAN member states, having joined only in 1999.[82] Only by looking back at history can one understand the nature of the problem. The Siamese and the Khmers are traditional foes. The kingdom of Angkor arose in the ninth century.[83] This kingdom exercised control over a territory that today extends into southern Laos and north-eastern Thailand. The temple dates from the eleventh century, though it can be traced back to a ninth-century hermitage founded by Prince Indrayudha, the son of King Jayavarman II.[84] From the thirteenth century Angkor was increasingly challenged by Thai kingdoms, principally Ayutthaya to the west. The borders shifted with the ebb and flow of

---

[81] Much of the authors' information comes from diplomatic sources and should therefore be treated with suitable caution. Any conclusions drawn are tentative and subject to revision when a more authoritative record of events is available.

[82] Cambodia's membership was delayed on account of the uncertain political situation following hostilities between supporters of the two co-Prime Ministers, Prince Norodom Ranariddh and Hun Sen. See the Joint Statement of the Special Meeting of the ASEAN Foreign Ministers on Cambodia (Kuala Lumpur, July 1997) and Severino, *Southeast Asia*, pp. 57–67. In reality, Hun Sen had launched a coup against his co-Prime Minister Prince Ranariddh.

[83] For a general introduction to the historical background, see M. Ricklefs et al., *A New History of Southeast Asia* (Palgrave Macmillan, Basingstoke, 2010), chaps. 3, 5 and 10.

[84] See the Historical Description on the UNESCO World Heritage List website: whc.unesco.org.

power of the competing polities. The temple complex of Angkor Wat and the city of Angkor Thom were eventually abandoned (though not forgotten, despite French claims to have 'discovered' the ruins in the nineteenth century) and the capital moved eastwards near the present-day Phnom Penh. The historic rivalry between Cambodia and Thailand lends a particular sensitivity to claims of sovereignty on that border. Siem Reap, where Cambodia's premier national symbol Angkor Wat is located, is roughly translated as 'Victory over Siam'. Even the false accusation that a Thai actress had questioned the sovereignty of Cambodia over Angkor Wat was sufficient to provoke anti-Thai riots in Phnom Penh in 2003.

The disputed border was demarcated in 1907 by a treaty between the Kingdom of Siam and the French colonial authorities who had control over Cambodia, a process which was not entirely accepted by the Thais. After the fall of France in 1940, Siam took the opportunity to regain the 'lost' territory in a short war against the French colonial authorities in 1941.[85] The end of the Pacific War saw the return of these territories to French control.[86] Despite this, Thailand occupied portions of

---

[85] See Britannica Online (www.britannica.com) under 'Thailand: The Phibun Dictatorship and World War II'.

[86] Thailand was allied to Japan. It managed nonetheless to escape post-war retribution beyond retrocession of territories taken from Burma, Malaya, Cambodia and Laos during the war. See Ricklefs et al., *A New History of Southeast Asia*, pp. 299–300, 360–2. France never accepted the forcible annexation by Thailand of the territories in French Indochina in 1941. These territories were retroceded in an accord dated 17 November 1946: see Annex VI to Cambodia's Application Instituting Proceedings in the *Case Concerning the Temple of Preah Vihear* (15 September 1959), p. 79, para. 2.

2.1 THE CURRENT REALITY

the Cambodian province of Kompong Thom, including Preah Vihear, in 1949.[87] Prince Norodom Sihanouk took control of Cambodia's government in 1952 and won recognition for an independent Cambodia at the Geneva Conference in 1954, which had been convened to reach a settlement of the First Indochina War.[88] That same year Thai troops occupied the ruins of Preah Vihear.[89]

In 1959 Cambodia instituted proceedings against Thailand in the International Court of Justice. Both countries had filed declarations accepting the compulsory jurisdiction of the court.[90] The original dispute about sovereignty was settled by the decision of the ICJ in 1962.[91] The ICJ held by nine votes to three that the temple stood in territory under the sovereignty of Cambodia. This judgment did not solve the problem, merely postponed the reckoning. The ICJ only trimmed the weeds without digging out the roots.

The dispute flared up again when Cambodia applied to have the ruins of Preah Vihear accepted as a UNESCO

---

[87] Para. 1 of the Application Instituting Proceedings in the *Case Concerning the Temple of Preah Vihear* (15 September 1959).
[88] See Britannica Online (www.britannica.com) under 'Cambodia: Independence'.
[89] Para. 1 of the Application Instituting Proceedings in the *Case Concerning the Temple of Preah Vihear* (15 September 1959).
[90] Thailand on 20 May 1950 and Cambodia on 19 September 1957. A check on the ICJ website (www.icj-cij.org) reveals that Thailand has withdrawn its declaration.
[91] *Case Concerning the Temple of Preah Vihear (Merits)*, judgment dated 15 June 1962.

World Heritage site in 2008.[92] Although Thailand under Prime Minister Thaksin Shinawatra and his successor was initially supportive, the issue became entangled in Thai domestic politics. Prime Minister Thaksin had been deposed by a coup in 2006 and his political foes used the Preah Vihear issue as a weapon to destabilise the government. The UNESCO listing took place in July 2008. In that same month an informal meeting of the ASEAN Foreign Ministers took place in Singapore, which held the Chair of ASEAN. Singapore's Foreign Minister George Yeo announced that the Foreign Ministers had placed ASEAN's facilities at the disposal of the parties for the settlement of the dispute.[93] A proposal was made for a Contact Group to support the parties in their effort to reach a peaceful resolution. However, the parties would not accept the assistance of their ASEAN colleagues at that time. Indeed, the Thai Foreign Minister stated that a constitutional amendment (introduced after the coup that deposed Prime Minister Thaksin Shinawatra) precluded him from negotiating territorial matters, on pain of being charged with treason. This constitutional prohibition was raised by successive Thai Foreign Ministers when pressed by their ASEAN colleagues to negotiate a settlement. Sporadic fighting broke out at the site from October 2008 to

---

[92] The background to this is recounted in International Crisis Group Asia Report No. 215, 'Waging Peace: ASEAN and the Thai–Cambodian Border Conflict' (6 December 2011), pp. 4–6, 9–12.

[93] See Statement by Singaporean Minister for Foreign Affairs George Yeo, 22 July 2008, available on the website of the Ministry of Foreign Affairs, Singapore: www.mfa.gov.sg.

2.1 THE CURRENT REALITY

early 2009.[94] Nothing moved during the chairmanship of Thailand the following year, as might be expected. The domestic political situation in Thailand remained extremely volatile.[95] Vietnam took over the chair of ASEAN in 2010. Cambodian Foreign Minister Hor Namhong wrote to Vietnamese Foreign Minister Pham Gia Khiem requesting mediation of the dispute but Thailand declined.[96] On 4 February 2011, in an escalation of the dispute, fighting broke out between Thailand and Cambodia in the vicinity of Preah Vihear.

ASEAN was lucky to have Indonesia in the chair at that time. It was pure serendipity; Brunei was supposed to have taken the chair of ASEAN, but had, at Indonesia's request, swapped slots. Indonesian Foreign Minister Marty Natalegawa was a seasoned diplomat. He had been Indonesia's Permanent Representative to the United Nations and Director-General in charge of ASEAN matters in the Indonesian Foreign Ministry and therefore was intimately familiar with how the system works. He was immediately on the phone to Cambodian Foreign Minister Hor Namhong and Thai Foreign Minister Kasit Piromya. On 7 and 8 February he was in Phnom Penh and Bangkok for talks. The Thais

---

[94] International Crisis Group Asia Report No. 215, 'Waging Peace: ASEAN and the Thai–Cambodian Border Conflict' (6 December 2011), p. 6.

[95] Clashes between different political factions had forced the cancellation of the ASEAN Summit that was to have been held in Pattaya in April, an enormous humiliation for Thailand. See BBC news, 11 April 2009, available on the website of the BBC: news.bbc.co.uk.

[96] International Crisis Group Asia Report No. 215, 'Waging Peace: ASEAN and the Thai–Cambodian Border Conflict' (6 December 2011), p. 15.

preferred to keep the dispute at a bilateral level. The Cambodians, no doubt calculating that they would be seen as the wronged party, insisted on bringing the matter to the UN Security Council.

On 14 February Indonesian Foreign Minister Marty Natalegawa, speaking as the Chair of ASEAN, told the United Nations Security Council (UNSC) that ASEAN wanted an observer mission. The UNSC, which had more pressing matters to deal with than a minor border skirmish in Southeast Asia, left it to ASEAN to sort out.[97] Armed with this mandate, Foreign Minister Natalegawa began shuttling between the disputing parties, as the Cambodian and Thai Foreign Ministers would not meet face-to-face. With the backing of the other ASEAN Foreign Ministers, he persuaded the Thais and the Cambodians that a continuing dispute would not be good for ASEAN solidarity. There were no threats of armed intervention, economic sanctions or even diplomatic isolation. The appeal was to enlightened self-interest. An informal (i.e., previously unscheduled) meeting of ASEAN Foreign Ministers was held on 22 February in Jakarta. Foreign Minister Natalegawa briefed the other ministers on the result of his visits to Phnom Penh and Bangkok and his appearance before the UNSC. Thai Foreign Minister Kasit Piromya and Cambodian Foreign Minister Hor Namhong presented their countries' respective positions.

---

[97] See the Press Release of the ASEAN Secretariat entitled 'Historic Firsts: ASEAN Efforts on Cambodian–Thai Conflict Endorsed by UNSC', 21 February 2011.

2.1 THE CURRENT REALITY

A statement was issued by the Foreign Ministers[98] welcoming Indonesia's efforts in her capacity as Chair of ASEAN and requesting that those efforts continue. The disputing parties accepted (with varying degrees of enthusiasm) the proposal that Indonesian observers be deployed on both sides of the border to prevent a resumption of hostilities. Singaporean Foreign Minister George Yeo shed some light on the manoeuvres behind the scenes when he answered a parliamentary question on 3 March 2011. He revealed that even though the Thais had been unwilling to accept Indonesian observers initially, faced with peer pressure from the other nine members they eventually relented.[99] The Foreign Ministers requested Indonesia to continue ASEAN's efforts to find a peaceful resolution of the dispute.

This unfortunately did not lead to the settlement of the problem. Although the Thai government may have agreed to accept Indonesian observers, the Thai military remained recalcitrant. The Cambodians pursued a parallel dispute settlement process, applying to the ICJ for interpretation of its 1962 judgment[100] and for provisional measures[101] on 28 April 2011. The ICJ pronounced its decision regarding

---

[98] Statement by the Chairman of ASEAN, 22 February 2011.
[99] See the Singapore Ministry of Foreign Affairs Press Release regarding Foreign Minister George Yeo's remarks in the Singapore Parliament, available on the website of the Ministry of Foreign Affairs, Singapore: www.mfa.gov.sg.
[100] Under Article 60 of the Statute of the Court and Article 98 of the Rules of Court.
[101] Under Article 41 of the Statute and Article 73 of the Rules.

provisional measures on 18 July 2011,[102] ordering both parties to withdraw their military personnel from a defined provisional demilitarised zone and refrain from taking any action to aggravate the situation. The parties were enjoined to 'continue the co-operation which they have entered into within ASEAN and, in particular, allow the observers appointed by that organization to have access to the provisional demilitarised zone'. The Indonesian observers were not deployed in the end. This was a matter of realpolitik rather than law. The primary object of ASEAN's intervention was to end the hostilities. Once the shooting stopped there was no further need. On 11 November 2013 the ICJ delivered judgment largely in favour of Cambodia while enjoining the parties to 'cooperate between themselves and with the international community in the protection of the site as a world heritage'.[103]

(2.1.3.2) Some general observations

Three key points emerge from the Preah Vihear saga.

First, recourse to a binding mode of dispute settlement is rare. It is vital to appreciate that recourse to arbitration or an international tribunal is a political decision, not a legal one. Unlike in the case of domestic dispute settlement, the complainant has to factor in the cost in terms of damage

---

[102] Request for the Interpretation of the Judgment of 15 June 1962 in the *Case Concerning the Temple of Preah Vihear,* Order dated 18 July 2011.

[103] Request for the Interpretation of the Judgment of 15 June 1962 in the *Case Concerning the Temple of Preah Vihear,* judgment dated 11 November 2013, para. 106.

2.1 THE CURRENT REALITY

to bilateral relations with the respondent[104] and possibly with other ASEAN states that may have urged the parties to come to an amicable settlement. The strength of the complainant's legal case is only one factor to be considered. It may not even be the decisive factor. Once a complainant crosses the Rubicon by invoking a binding dispute settlement mechanism, the die is cast; anything short of victory means a loss of face and domestic political credibility. Where the government is weak domestically, political opponents can hijack nationalistic sentiments for short-term political advantage. Only a secure government can afford to run the political risk; ironically, a democratic government facing elections or dependent on coalition partners may be less willing to resort to binding international dispute settlement than an authoritarian regime.

While nationalism may have decreased somewhat in Western Europe, to which ASEAN is often compared, in Southeast Asia it is most certainly not dead. The colonial interlude kept the regional disputes in check. The Preah Vihear case reminds us that these problems still fester. The disagreement over Preah Vihear became a piece in a rowdy

---

[104] In the Preah Vihear case bilateral relations between the disputing parties were at a low ebb when reference was made to the ICJ. At one point the Cambodian government appointed ousted Thai Prime Minister Thaksin Shinawatra as adviser to Prime Minister Hun Sen, a move that could only have been calculated to irritate the Thais. See International Crisis Group Asia Report No. 215, 'Waging Peace: ASEAN and the Thai–Cambodian Border Conflict' (6 December 2011), pp. 12–13. Relations have improved since the election of the new government under Thaksin's sister Yingluck.

game of domestic political one-upmanship in Thailand.[105] Governments may be willing to be bound by international norms, but they may be constrained by domestic politics in what they can do. A strong military with a history of political interventionism does not help. The Philippine/Thailand WTO case[106] provides a sharp contrast. That matter arose at almost exactly the same time. Thailand lost the case and agreed to implement the decision of the WTO Dispute Settlement Body. This was possible because the matter did not become enmeshed in the web of Thai domestic politics.

The Preah Vihear case is the first to have arisen after the coming into operation of the Charter. ASEAN member states had previously brought boundary disputes to the ICJ on two occasions: the Ligitan/Sipadan case between Indonesia and Malaysia in 1998[107] and the Pedra Branca case between Malaysia and Singapore in 2003.[108] Both of these cases might have been dealt with under the TAC, but, as has been pointed out above, that procedure is more political than judicial. The submission of the Ligitan/Sipadan dispute to the ICJ was a decision taken at the highest level, despite the reservations of

---

[105] The political background is explained in detail in the International Crisis Group Asia Report No. 215, 'Waging Peace: ASEAN and the Thai–Cambodian Border Conflict' (6 December 2011).
[106] Dispute DS371, discussed above.
[107] *Case Concerning Sovereignty over Pulau Ligitan and Pulau Sipadan*, judgment dated 17 December 2002.
[108] *Case Concerning Sovereignty over Pedra Branca/Pulau Batu Puteh, Middle Rocks and South Ledge*, judgment dated 23 May 2008.

2.1 THE CURRENT REALITY

officials.[109] Interestingly, in submitting the dispute to the ICJ the parties explicitly referred to the TAC.[110] Similarly, the Pedra Branca case was submitted to the court after negotiations had proven unsuccessful. In both instances there was sufficient political will to have the matter resolved finally by adjudication.[111] It is probably no coincidence that in both cases the governments of the disputants were secure and did not face domestic political instability.

The Preah Vihear case is different in that it reached the court at the instance of only one party; Thailand was opposed to the process. Thailand's reluctance can be

---

[109] Indonesia had tried to bring the Ligitan/Sipadan dispute to the High Council under the TAC but Malaysia refused, fearing that other ASEAN members would be partial to Indonesia: see Severino, *Southeast Asia*, pp. 12–13. President Soeharto decided to submit the dispute to the ICJ, overriding the objections of his officials.

[110] The Special Agreement (signed 31 May 1997 by the Foreign Ministers of the two countries, viz., Mr Ali Alatas and Datuk Abdullah Badawi) stated in the preamble that the parties desired 'that this dispute should be settled in the spirit of friendly relations existing between the Parties as enunciated in the 1976 Treaty of Amity and Cooperation in Southeast Asia'.

[111] Singapore and Malaysia have been particularly assiduous in using third-party adjudication mechanisms to settle disputes. Singapore invoked the WTO Dispute Settlement Mechanism against Malaysia in 1995: see Dispute DS1; the complaint was eventually withdrawn when the underlying cause of complaint was redressed. On 5 September 2003 Malaysia submitted a Request for Provisional Measures to the International Tribunal on Law of the Sea (ITLOS) in relation to Singapore's land reclamation activities near their common maritime boundary: see *Case Concerning Land Reclamation by Singapore in and around the Straits of Johor*. The parties came to a settlement of their differences.

explained in a large part by the volatility of its domestic politics.[112] However, the procedure under Article 60 of the Statute of the ICJ allows one party to request interpretation and that was sufficient for the court to be seised of the matter despite the opposition of the Thais.

Second point: the three ICJ cases highlight the weakness of the adjudication process, at least where territorial delimitation is the issue. It is a zero-sum game. There is always a loser. The loss may rankle a generation after the court decision, as the Preah Vihear case demonstrates. The loser loses face. That is not desirable in an ASEAN context, the *raison d'être* of ASEAN being to foster trust among the member states. The reluctance to submit territorial disputes to binding adjudication is not confined to ASEAN, as the current spat between South Korea and Japan over Takeshima/Dokdo demonstrates. Moreover, it often happens that the loser then decides that it will never again be placed in such a position.[113] This is again not a phenomenon unique to ASEAN. When the ICJ ruled against Colombia in a recent

---

[112] See the International Crisis Group Asia Report No. 215, 'Waging Peace: ASEAN and the Thai–Cambodian Border Conflict' (6 December 2011), pp. 11–12, 21–22.

[113] Thailand had at one time submitted to the compulsory jurisdiction of the International Court of Justice. A check on the website of the ICJ (www.icj-cij.org) reveals that the Declaration of Thailand recognising compulsory jurisdiction of the ICJ filed on 20 May 1950 appears to have been withdrawn. During the negotiations on the drafting of the ASEAN Charter, Indonesia was keen on not creating a compulsory dispute settlement mechanism. One can only speculate as to the underlying motives in these two examples, but it is probably a fair inference that being on the losing side in the Preah Vihear and Ligitan/Sipadan cases

2.1 THE CURRENT REALITY

case on territorial delimitation,[114] the latter reacted by withdrawing from the Pact of Bogotá,[115] under which it had accepted the compulsory jurisdiction of the court.

The ASEAN way is to seek compromise, using the Charter and peer pressure as levers. On Armistice Day 2013 the ICJ clarified its 1962 judgment on Preah Vihear. Thailand was obliged to withdraw its forces from the promontory of Preah Vihear and ensure access to the Temple from the Cambodian side.[116] One wonders whether the second pronouncement will have any greater effect than the first in dealing with the roots of the dispute. More promising would be the efforts within ASEAN to find a solution that does not result in a loss of face for one party; a possibility would be some sort of joint cooperation to exploit the potential of the area. When two neighbours argue about the ownership of a durian tree, it does not make any sense to let the durians fall and rot on the ground while they try to settle their differences.

What of the ASEAN Charter provisions? At the time that the dispute arose the 2010 Protocol had already been signed, though it was not yet in force. The weakness of the

---

respectively played a part in shaping these countries' attitudes towards compulsory jurisdiction in the settlement of inter-state disputes.

[114] *Territorial and Maritime Dispute (Nicaragua v. Colombia)*, judgment dated 19 November 2012.

[115] American Treaty on Pacific Settlement, in force 6 May 1949. Colombia was one of the original signatories on 30 April 1948. It denounced the treaty on 27 November 2012. It was reported that Colombia's President had said, 'Never again should we have to face what happened to us on November 19': *The Economist*, 8–14 December 2012, p. 55.

[116] Request for the Interpretation of the Judgment of 15 June 1962 in the *Case Concerning the Temple of Preah Vihear*, judgment dated 11 November 2013.

Charter is that there is no mechanism to force a settlement of any dispute. Recourse to the TAC is provided for in Article 24(2) of the Charter, but the TAC mechanism is voluntary. Even if it were mandatory, the TAC route would not produce a legally binding result.

This leads to the third major point: the existence of the ASEAN Charter gave the ASEAN Chair the cover needed to attempt to effect a peaceful resolution of disputes. This happened both in 2008 when Singapore held the Chair and in 2011 when Indonesia was the incumbent. The first attempt by Singaporean Foreign Minister George Yeo proved abortive in the face of resistance by the disputants; one cannot force unwilling parties to compromise, short of sending in troops or imposing sanctions. This is not practical in an ASEAN context, or indeed in any international context.[117] The second attempt by Indonesian Foreign Minister Marty Natalegawa to broker a deal in his capacity as ASEAN Chair was more successful. Faced with peer pressure from the other nine, the Thais agreed to accept the Indonesian suggestion for the deployment of observers. Whatever the exact words of the Charter may be, it is clear that the actions of the Chair were considered to be fully in accordance with the spirit of the treaty. The Statement issued after the informal Foreign

---

[117] Those who complain about the ineffectiveness of the ASEAN way should ask whether the international community has been any more successful in brokering peace among unwilling parties over the last half century. One need only mention the current situation in Syria and the Israeli-occupied territories on the West Bank.

2.1 THE CURRENT REALITY

Ministers' meeting[118] explicitly referred to the TAC and the Charter as the basis for the intervention of the Chair in the dispute.

The Preah Vihear case is illuminating also because it demonstrates graphically the limitations under which a politically appointed Secretary-General works. The incumbent Secretary-General, Dr Surin Pitsuwan, had been Foreign Minister of Thailand in the past and was a member of the ruling Democrat Party. He clearly could not be a neutral interlocutor in a case between his country and Cambodia.[119] However, this was a problem not with the office of the Secretary-General as such but rather with the person who held the post. Under the Charter disputing parties may request the Secretary-General to provide good offices, conciliation or mediation.[120] The same is true under the Vientiane Protocol.[121] Potentially, the Secretary-General can play a pivotal role in the settlement of disputes within ASEAN. A Secretary-General who is perceived to be impartial and not beholden to his country of origin could have considerable influence in bringing disputing parties together. So much depends on the personalities involved, however.

---

[118] Statement issued by the Chairman after the Informal Meeting of the Foreign Ministers of ASEAN on 22 February 2011.
[119] When asked how he might assist in resolving the dispute, Dr Surin reportedly quipped, 'This is a dispute between two Buddhist countries over a Hindu temple. What can I, a Muslim, do?'
[120] ASEAN Charter, Article 23(2).
[121] 2004 ASEAN Protocol on Enhanced Dispute Settlement Mechanism, Article 4(3). Under this provision the Secretary-General may offer his services; he does not have to wait to be asked.

2.2 Building the ASEAN Community

Ever since Bali Concord II in 2003 the stated ambition of the member states has been to create an ASEAN Community based on three pillars: the ASEAN Economic Community (AEC), the ASEAN Political-Security Community (APSC) and the ASEAN Socio-Cultural Community (ASCC). Over the following years there have been constant references to a 'rules-based' community. Before discussing the need for an ASEAN Legal Service in the next chapter, it is useful to appreciate the level of integration contemplated by the member states.

2.2.1 *The Community Blueprints*

ASEAN's progress towards the creation of a Community will not be linear. It is more likely to resemble a waltz, with the various member states, organs and other parties meandering all around the dance floor trying to keep in harmony. The Community Blueprints provide the background music.

First off was the Blueprint for the ASEAN Economic Community (AEC), adopted on 20 November 2007 at the Thirteenth ASEAN Summit in Singapore. This is designed to transform ASEAN into a single market and production base by 2015. This comprises five core elements,[122] namely, free flow of goods, investments, services and skilled labour and a freer flow of capital. The free flow of goods necessitates not only the reduction of tariffs but also the elimination of

---

[122] 2007 ASEAN Economic Community Blueprint, para. 9.

2.2 BUILDING THE ASEAN COMMUNITY

non-tariff barriers.[123] The member states pledge to work towards having regional rules and regulations consistent with international best practices.[124] A regional trade facilitation cooperation mechanism is also to be established.[125] Technical standards are to be harmonised.[126] In the area of investment, the member states are to strengthen investor–state dispute settlement mechanisms.[127] Greater capital mobility and harmonisation of capital market standards is promised.[128] Efforts to combat illegal logging and fishing are to be strengthened.[129] In the area of intellectual property rights member states are to establish an ASEAN filing system for design.[130] To encourage e-commerce the legal infrastructure for electronic contracting and dispute resolution is to be harmonised.[131]

The ASEAN Political-Security Community (APSC) Blueprint was adopted at the Fourteenth ASEAN Summit in Cha-am, Thailand on 1 March 2009. This envisaged the creation of a 'rules-based community of shared values and norms'.[132] In concrete terms, ASEAN member states are to intensify cooperation on combating corruption,[133] transnational crime,[134] trafficking of people,[135] drug trafficking,[136] cyber-crime[137] and terrorism.[138]

---

[123] Ibid., para. 11. [124] Ibid., para. 14.v. [125] Ibid., para. 16.iv.
[126] Ibid., para. 19. [127] Ibid., para. 27. [128] Ibid., paras. 31 and 32.
[129] Ibid., para. 39.iv and v. [130] Ibid., para. 45.ii. [131] Ibid., para. 59.ii.
[132] 2009 ASEAN Political-Security Community Blueprint, para. 10.
[133] Ibid., para. A.1.7. [134] Ibid., para. B.4.1. [135] Ibid., para. B.4.1.iv.
[136] Ibid., para. B.4.1.vi. [137] Ibid., para. B.4.1.xvi.
[138] Ibid., para. B.4.2.

The Fourteenth ASEAN Summit also adopted the ASEAN Socio-Cultural Community (ASCC) Blueprint. This is the most wide-ranging of the three pillars. Several areas stand out from the perspective of legal regulation: harmonisation of food safety regulations (including procedures for the movement of plants, animals and their products),[139] strengthened cooperation in health quarantine,[140] establishment of an ASEAN commission for the promotion and protection of the rights of women and children,[141] protection of the rights of migrant workers[142] and regulation of recruitment of migrant workers by sending states.[143] Environmental protection is one of the main areas of focus. Transboundary trade in wild flora and fauna is to be more effectively regulated.[144] Member states are to strengthen the enforcement of laws for the sustainable management of forests and combating of illegal logging.[145]

The preceding non-exhaustive list of measures to realise the ASEAN Community gives some idea of the scale of ambition. None of this can come to pass without a proper legal basis.

---

[139] Ibid., para. 21.i. The SARS crisis of 2003 left a mark on the collective consciousness of ASEAN member states. Combating avian influenza remains a priority concern.
[140] Ibid., para. 23.xi.
[141] Ibid., para. 27.i. It was reported at the Twenty-first ASEAN Summit (Phnom Penh, November 2012) that the Commission was finalising its five-year work plan for 2012–16.
[142] 2009 ASEAN Socio-Cultural Community Blueprint, para. 28.i.
[143] Ibid., para. 28.viii.   [144] Ibid., para. 38.xi.
[145] Ibid., para. 41.x and xi.

2.2 BUILDING THE ASEAN COMMUNITY

2.2.2 Bali Concord III and the ASEAN Human Rights Declaration

At the Nineteenth ASEAN Summit in Bali (November 2011) the leaders adopted the Bali Declaration on ASEAN Community in a Global Community of Nations (Bali Concord III). This document declared that ASEAN would have a 'common platform' on global issues by 2022. The ASEAN Coordinating Council (ACC) comprising the Foreign Ministers were put in charge. The ACC is to be supported by the relevant senior officials, the Committee of Permanent Representatives and an enhanced ASEAN Secretariat with the capacity to 'provide effective support in projecting ASEAN's collective undertakings at the global level'.

The core concept is that ASEAN's position on global issues should be better coordinated and more coherent. It appears that ASEAN's ambition is to be a serious player on the world stage. The leitmotiv of ASEAN as a rules-based organisation is reiterated once again. As far as the APSC is concerned, the peaceful settlement of disputes is once again emphasised.[146] There is also a commitment to promote and protect human rights and fundamental freedoms.[147] The goal of economic integration is underlined. Within the sphere of the ASCC there are commitments to better coordination and cooperation in disaster management and environmental protection.

The year following Bali Concord III, ASEAN finally adopted the ASEAN Human Rights Declaration (AHRD) at

---

[146] 2011 Bali Declaration on ASEAN Community in a Global Community of Nations (Bali Concord III), para. A.1.
[147] Ibid., para. A.2.b.

the Twenty-first ASEAN Summit in Phnom Penh (November 2012). This represents a major milestone for ASEAN. Human rights was the one issue that nearly derailed the drafting of the ASEAN Charter in 2007. The AHRD sets out the human rights of all citizens of ASEAN member states. There is a pledge to promote and protect human rights through cooperation among the member states as well as with national, regional and international institutions and organisations.[148]

Bali Concord III and the ASEAN Human Rights Declaration, together with the ASEAN Charter, fundamentally alter the way ASEAN has worked for four decades after its foundation. There is a clearly declared ambition to form an integrated community based on the rule of law. Cynics might characterise all this as empty rhetoric. But aspirations are important for ASEAN. They provide a goal to aim for. The transformation of ASEAN into a rules-based organisation is a generational project. Progress may be slow, but there is movement in the right direction. One should not expect that progress will be linear; backsliding will occur. The constant public affirmation of the rule of law, protection of human rights and peaceful settlement of disputes as core principles of ASEAN allows peer pressure to be brought upon any member state that strays from the declared norm. The workings of ASEAN are not a Shakespearean drama full of sound and fury signifying nothing. It is more an Indonesian *wayang kulit*; behind the shadows on the screen the *dalang* are working quietly to move the story along. The challenge is to build the institutions that will make all of this function in practice.

[148] 2012 ASEAN Human Rights Declaration, Article 39.

Chapter 3

The ASEAN Legal Service

The first two chapters of this monograph have set out the history and structure of ASEAN in order to enable the reader to understand the current reality. This is the essential context within which to consider the role of a putative ASEAN Legal Service. However, before proceeding to deal with ASEAN, it is instructive to look at how other international organisations have organised their legal services.

3.1 The European Union

Though ASEAN has sometimes been compared with the EU, it is clear that the ASEAN Legal Service cannot be directly based on the model of the legal services of the institutions of the EU.

3.1.1 *The EU legal order*

The EU has established a new legal order which differs widely from classic public international law.[1] The institutions of the EU are part of a very sophisticated and integrated system of law.

---

[1] Short reminder of important dates in the history of the European Union (EU):

1954: the six founding states (Belgium, France, Germany, Italy, Luxembourg and the Netherlands) establish the European Coal and Steel Community (ECSC).

As one of the authors of this book wrote in 1999:

in very simple terms, the present situation might be described as follows: the EU has law-making institutions, including a Council composed of Ministers who are members of national governments of the member states, and a directly elected European Parliament. The Council and the Parliament share the power of co-deciding legislative, administrative and budgetary acts, which are proposed by the Commission. The Commission, which exercises the powers conferred on it by the Council for the implementation of (EU) law, also ensures that this law is applied and may take a member state to Court if it fails to fulfil its obligations. The Parliament shares with the member states the power to approve the appointment of the President of the Commission and of the Commission as a whole; the Parliament has also the power to remove

1958: the same six states establish also the European Economic Community (EEC)
1973: accession of Denmark, Ireland and the United Kingdom
1981: accession of Greece
1986: accession of Portugal and Spain
1987: Single European Act (SEA)
1993: Maastricht Treaty on the European Union (TEU)
1995: accession of Austria, Finland and Sweden
1999: Amsterdam Treaty
2003: Nice Treaty
2004: accession of Cyprus, Czech Republic, Estonia, Hungary, Latvia, Lithuania, Malta, Poland, Slovakia and Slovenia
2005: failure of the Constitutional Treaty
2007: accession of Bulgaria and Romania
2009: Treaty of Lisbon, the EU is based on the Treaty on European Union (TEU) and on the Treaty on the Functioning of the European Union (TFEU)
2013: accession of Croatia, the EU has twenty-eight member states.

3.1 THE EUROPEAN UNION

the Commission from office. The laws adopted by these institutions within the fields of power of the (EU) are superior to the laws of the member states and may have direct effects on the citizens of the Union. The Union has a single market and manages a single currency and monetary union for most of its Member States. There are a number of fields for which the Member States have lost power to adopt legislation and to negotiate international agreements. There are other fields where 'laws' (regulations and directives) or treaties can be imposed on the Member States and which they are obliged to implement, or else being faced with having to make lump sums or penalty payments, as well as paying compensation to adversely affected people. The Court of Justice has the power to rule on disputes between the institutions, between institutions and Member States about the extent of their respective powers, and on the rights and obligations of Member States and citizens under European law. This 'new legal order' is embodied in fundamental texts which define these institutions and their powers, and oblige them to respect the rule of law and human rights.[2]

As the preceding chapters have abundantly demonstrated, ASEAN is very far from presenting characteristics close to those of the EU. The EU is partly 'supra-national', as its member states have accepted to share some of their sovereign powers. This is not the case for ASEAN. In a similar way, EU law is different from classic public international law, on which ASEAN law is based. Obviously, there is no principle of

---

[2] Jean-Claude Piris, 'Does the EU Have a Constitution? Does It Need One?', *European Law Review* 24 (1999): 557.

primacy or supremacy of ASEAN law over the national law of its member states, and there is no possible direct applicability or effect of ASEAN law. There is no possibility of an infringement procedure against a member state in a Court of Justice, and no possibility of any preliminary ruling on request from a national court, as there is not any ASEAN Court of Justice.

The infringement procedure is one means of securing compliance with EU law (Box 3.1). Another means is the preliminary ruling procedure (Box 3.2).

Box 3.1 The infringement procedure

This is an essential feature of the EU legal order, which distinguishes it from public international law.

Article 4(3) (second subparagraph) TEU provides:

> The member states shall take any appropriate measure, general or particular, to ensure fulfilment of the obligations arising out of the Treaties or resulting from the acts of the institutions of the Union.

Article 17(1) TEU provides:

> The Commission ... shall ensure the application of the Treaties, and of the measures adopted by the institutions pursuant to them. It shall oversee the application of Union law under the control of the Court of Justice of the EU.

Article 258 TFEU provides:

> If the Commission considers that a Member State has failed to fulfil an obligation under the Treaties, it

shall deliver a reasoned opinion on the matter after giving the State concerned the opportunity to submit its observations.

If the State concerned does not comply with the opinion within the period laid down by the Commission, the latter may bring the matter before the Court of Justice of the EU.

Article 260 TFEU provides:

1. If the Court of Justice of the European Union finds that a Member State has failed to fulfil an obligation under the Treaties, the State shall be required to take the necessary measures to comply with the judgment of the Court.

2. If the Commission considers that the Member State concerned has not taken the necessary measures to comply with the judgment of the Court, it may bring the case before the Court after giving that State the opportunity to submit its observations. It shall specify the amount of the lump sum or penalty payment to be paid by the Member State concerned which it considers appropriate in the circumstances.

   If the Court finds that the Member State concerned has not complied with its judgment it may impose a lump sum or penalty payment on it.

The possibility of requiring a member state to pay a lump sum or a penalty was introduced in the Treaties by the entry into force of the Maastricht Treaty in 1993. The first

THE ASEAN LEGAL SERVICE

> **Box 3.1** (cont.)
>
> time the Court of Justice used that possibility was in July 2005, when the Court ordered a member state to pay both a penalty payment and a lump sum for serious and persistent failure to comply with Community law.[3] That judgment, together with the Commission Communication of 15 January 2011,[4] makes it clear that member states which do not comply with EU law face substantial financial sanctions. It acts as a powerful deterrent and reduces the need to go to the end of the Article 260 procedure. Moreover, the entry into force of the Lisbon Treaty at the end of 2009 brought important changes in infringement management. One change is the possibility for the Commission to request, at an early stage, financial sanctions against a member state failing to notify measures transposing a directive (see annual reports from the Commission on the Monitoring of the Application of EU Law). That explains why the number of cases reaching the final step in the infringement procedure is regularly decreasing: fifty-four cases were brought before the Court by the Commission in 2012, instead of seventy in 2011 and 120 in 2010, in constant decline since 2008 (210 cases).

---

[3] Judgment of the EU Court of Justice, 12 July 2005; Case C-304/02 *Commission v. France*, European Court Reports 2005, p. I-06263.

[4] *Official Journal of the EU*, 15 January 2011, C12/1.

3.1 THE EUROPEAN UNION

> **Box 3.2** The preliminary ruling procedure
>
> This is another aspect where the EU legal order distinguishes itself from public international law. Besides presenting the specific characteristics of 'supremacy', 'direct applicability' and 'direct effect', the EU legal order is also characterised by its 'uniformity of interpretation'. This uniformity is the responsibility of the Court of Justice.
>
> According to Article 267 TFEU:
>
>> The Court of Justice of the European Union shall have jurisdiction to give preliminary rulings concerning:
>>
>> (a) the interpretation of the Treaties;
>> (b) the validity and interpretation of acts of the institutions, bodies, offices or agencies of the Union;
>>
>> Where such a question is raised before any court or tribunal of a Member State, that court or tribunal may, if it considers that a decision on the question is necessary to enable it to give judgment, request the Court to give a ruling thereon.
>>
>> Where any such question is raised in a case pending before a court or tribunal of a Member State against whose decisions there is no judicial remedy under national law, that court or tribunal shall bring the matter before the Court.
>>
>> If such a question is raised in a case pending before a court or tribunal of a Member State with regard to a

Box 3.2 (cont.)

person in custody, the Court of Justice of the European Union shall act with the minimum of delay.

The system of preliminary rulings reflects the fact that all national courts in the member states share the responsibility for applying EU law. To ensure that EU law is applied uniformly in all the member states, Article 267 TFEU *allows* all lower courts in the member states and *obliges* their Supreme Courts to refer questions of interpretation of EU law to the Court of Justice for a preliminary ruling. The Commission always intervenes in such proceedings to submit to the Court its observations on the interpretation of the relevant EU law provisions.

The meaning of the preliminary ruling system in the legal order of the EU was emphasised by the Court of Justice in its Report to the 1996 Inter-Governmental Conference in these terms:

> The development of the Community legal order has been to a large extent the fruit of the dialogue which has built up between the national courts and the Court of Justice through the preliminary ruling procedure. It is through such cooperation that the essential characteristics of the Community legal order have been identified, in particular its primacy over the laws of the Member States, the direct effect of a whole series of provisions and the right of individuals to obtain redress when their rights are infringed by a breach of

3.1 THE EUROPEAN UNION

> Community law for which a Member State is responsible. To limit access to the court would have the effect of jeopardizing the uniform application and interpretation of Community law throughout the Union, and could deprive individuals of effective judicial protection and undermine the unity of the case-law.
>
> But that is not all. The preliminary ruling system is the veritable cornerstone of the operation of the internal market, since it plays a fundamental role in ensuring that the law established by the treaties retains its Community character with a view to guaranteeing that that law has the same effect in all circumstances in all the Member States of the European Union. *Any weakening, even if only potential, of the uniform application and interpretation of Community law throughout the Union would be liable to give rise to distortions of competition and discrimination between economic operators, thus jeopardizing equality of opportunity as between those operators and consequently the proper functioning of the internal market.*[5]
>
> One of the Court's essential tasks is to ensure just such a uniform interpretation, and it discharges that duty by answering the questions put to it by the national courts and tribunals.[6]

---

[5] Outlined by one of the authors of this book.
[6] May 1995: http://europa.eu.int/en/agenda/igc-home/eu-doc/justice/cj_ep.html.

3.1.2 The Legal Services of the Commission and of the Council of the EU

(3.1.2.1) The Legal Service of the Commission[7]

The Legal Service of the Commission is an influential internal department reporting directly to the President of the Commission. Its role is twofold:

(i) to provide legal advice to the Commission and its services; and
(ii) to represent the Commission in all court cases.

The Commission's legal adviser

The Legal Service is associated with all preparatory work on acts of the Commission, with the aim of ensuring the legal coherence of policies and the legality of decisions. In addition, it assures the legislative quality of EU acts through its involvement in relevant projects before decisions are taken by the College. It is also in charge of the simplification of existing legislation, particularly through codification and recasting. Furthermore, as already mentioned, the Legal Service is a key player when the Commission exercises its role as 'guardian of the Treaties' in the management of infringement procedures under Articles 258 and 260 TFEU.

The Legal Service participates in all College meetings, in preparatory meetings, in other weekly meetings

---

[7] This part is based on the Annual Report of the Legal Service of the European Commission for the year 2012 (document of the Commission LS_aar_2012_final).

3.1 THE EUROPEAN UNION

of the Cabinets and in numerous meetings with other Directorates-General (DGs) and agencies of the institutions. In its role as legal adviser to the departments of the Commission – about forty-four DGs and Services – the Legal Service delivers opinions on legal questions. The DGs and Services must consult the Legal Service on all matters having legal implications and on all draft acts (in particular regulations, directives and decisions) before adoption by the Commission.

The Legal Service advises on compliance with EU law – the Treaties, general principles and basic legislation – and international obligations. In the case of draft acts, the Legal Service checks both the substantive legality and the drafting quality. The former covers such questions as: is the act legally correct? Is there any contradiction with the Treaties, case law and other legislation in force? The check of the quality of drafting ensures that all the formal rules are complied with and that provisions are drafted clearly and precisely. There is growing recognition that the quality of drafting is of utmost importance if both businesses and citizens in Europe are to be able to read and understand European law easily. The better regulation strategy which is consistently high on the agenda of the European Council shows that member states and the EU institutions are all concerned that EU legislation should be accessible, effective and simple, as well as being clearly and precisely drafted.

The independent legal advice provided by the Legal Service ensures that the Commission's decisions are substantively lawful and formally correct. This is of vital importance in preventing or reducing the risk of subsequent litigation. The opinion of the Legal Service carries considerable weight. A negative opinion can generally only be 'overruled' by a political decision of the full Commission and so DGs will make every effort to find a solution acceptable to the Legal Service. The Director-General of the Legal Service attends the weekly meetings of the full Commission (the 'College') to ensure that legal advice is available.

The legal advice provided by the Legal Service to another Commission department is an internal Commission document which is protected by Article 4 of Regulation (EC) No 1049/2001 regarding public access to European Parliament, Council and Commission documents.[8] The specific function and nature of opinions of the Legal Services of the institutions were recognised and confirmed by the General Court (formerly Court of First Instance) in a judgment of 23 November 2004 in a case concerning an opinion of the Council's Legal Service.[9]

The Commission Legal Service issues about 13,000–14,000 formal opinions every year. In many other cases it provides advice on an informal basis. This task of providing the Commission and its departments with legal advice, which is a major part of the Legal Service's activity, is of primary importance and might be seen as preventive work, in contrast to its other activity – litigation.

---

[8] *Official Journal L* 145, 31 May 2001, p. 43.
[9] Judgment of the Court of First Instance of 23 November 2004 in case T-84/03 *Maurizio Turco* v. *Council*, European Court Reports 2004, p. II-04061.

3.1 THE EUROPEAN UNION

The Commission's legal representative

The Legal Service represents the Commission before the courts: first, the three instances within the Court of Justice of the EU – namely the Court of Justice, the General Court and the Civil Service Tribunal; then the dispute settlement bodies within the WTO; and, finally, the national courts, both in the member states and in third countries, in cases where the EU or the Commission are parties (forced recovery of debts represents more than 60 percent of national cases).

The Legal Service role of legal representation of the Commission is exclusive. In addition, in the handling of litigation, Legal Service members must be present in all hearings before the three instances of the Court of Justice of the EU and before the WTO dispute settlement bodies. In 2012 the Legal Service has defended the interests of the Commission or the EU itself in 1,099 new cases before the courts of the EU, 129 before national courts and twenty-eight at the WTO. These cases are in addition to those initiated in previous years and still ongoing in 2012 (1,999 in the courts of the EU, about 800 before national courts and twenty-eight in the WTO).

In accordance with the Rules of Procedure of the Court of Justice, the lawyers of the Commission submit their written comments in whichever language is designated the language of the case. The Legal Service is composed of lawyers drawn from all the twenty-eight member states, thus ensuring availability of knowledge of all legal systems and all official languages of the EU.

The Commission may appear before the courts either as applicant (for example, in proceedings against member states for infringement of EU law) or as defendant (for example, in proceedings for annulment of a Commission act brought by a member state, an institution or a person). The Commission also often intervenes in proceedings involving another institution.

Overall, the Commission wins some 72 percent of its cases before the EU courts. Of course, the distinction between 'won' and 'lost' is not always clear-cut. Some cases are won in part and others won as to the principle but lost on formal grounds.

The organisation of the Legal Service of the Commission

The Legal Service of the Commission employed some 450 staff in 2013. It is organised in twelve 'thematic teams', ranging in size from under ten to over twenty specialist lawyers, which cover the policies and activities of one or more DG. They are each headed by a Principal Legal Adviser, equivalent to a Director, and they report to the Director-General.

The Quality of Legislation team, also headed by a Principal Legal Advisor, comprises the Legal Revisers Group and the Codification Group and altogether totals about eighty lawyers.

Finally there are administrative support groups such as Human Resources, and Information and Information Technology.

The internal organisation of the Legal Service is somewhat different from the organisation of a conventional Commission DG. It is more flexible and enables it to react quickly to defend the Commission's interests effectively.

3.1 THE EUROPEAN UNION

(3.1.2.2) The Legal Service of the EU Council

The EU has been conferred in the founding Treaties the power to legislate in a number of domains. The EU Council is made up of the representatives of the governments of the member states at ministerial level, each authorised to commit their government. The Council adopts EU legislation on the basis of a proposal by the European Commission, in most cases acting together with the European Parliament under the 'normal legislative procedure', which requires a co-decision between the Parliament and the Council. In matters of common foreign and security policy, the adoption of legislative acts is excluded, and the European Council and the Council have the responsibility to adopt decisions.

EU legislation has primacy over the law of the member states, and is in some cases directly applicable without the need for transposition into national legislation. The legality of EU legislation is subject to review by the Court of Justice of the EU. The Council therefore needs an independent legal service to help it respect the rule of law, on which the EU is founded, and to defend the Council in case of legal challenge. The Legal Service is part of the General Secretariat of the Council. It is also the Legal Service of the European Council, where the member states are represented by their Heads of State or Government.

The independence and professional quality of the Council's Legal Service are recognised by all member states and EU institutions.

THE ASEAN LEGAL SERVICE

Official Mission Statement of the Council's Legal Service

1. The Legal Service is the legal adviser to the Council and the European Council.
2. It assists the European Council, the Council and its preparatory bodies, the Presidency, and the General Secretariat, in order to ensure the legality and the drafting quality of legal acts. It contributes, by taking a creative approach where appropriate, to identifying legally correct and politically acceptable solutions, in cooperation with other Council departments. To that end, it gives opinions in complete impartiality – orally or in writing, at the request of the Council or on its own initiative – on any question of a legal nature.
3. The Legal Service also represents the European Council and the Council in proceedings before the courts of the EU.
4. The Legal Service is responsible for checking the drafting quality of legal acts of the European Council and the Council and ensuring that they are legally and linguistically consistent in all of the Union's official languages.
5. The constant objective of the Legal Service is to provide timely contributions which are distinguished by their full respect for the law, their impartiality and their clarity.

Organisation of the Council's Legal Service

The Council's Legal Service is under the responsibility of a Director-General, who is the Council's Legal Counsel. Among the 275 people working in the Legal Service, there are about fifty Legal Advisors, working in five Legal Directorates, in which nationals from almost all member states are represented. The

3.1 THE EUROPEAN UNION

Legal Advisors give legal advice to the Council and its preparatory bodies, and represent the Council in litigation before the EU courts. There is also a Directorate responsible for the Quality of Legislation with about one hundred 'lawyer-linguists'.

The Legal Directorates have the following areas of responsibility:

- Directorate I: internal market, energy, research, transport, social affairs, environment, consumer protection, competition and public procurement.
- Directorate II: agriculture and fisheries, economic and monetary union, tax matters, free movement of capital and structural funds.
- Directorate III: external relations, including CFSP, development cooperation, trade policy and enlargement.
- Directorate IV: institutional, budgetary and administrative questions.
- Directorate V: justice and home affairs.

Opinions of the Council's Legal Service

The advisory role of the Legal Service consists of giving legal opinions, either orally or in writing, to the European Council and to the Council and its preparatory bodies, on any legal or institutional questions which may be raised in the course of the deliberations. Even in cases when the Legal Service is not asked for an opinion, it is expected to draw attention to legal or institutional problems on its own initiative.

Opinions of the Legal Service may be given on issues such as whether the proposal which is discussed does fall within the competences conferred on the EU by the Treaties, as the Union would not have the power to intervene otherwise. The Legal Service must also check if the Commission has chosen the correct legal basis in the Treaty for a draft legislative act, international agreement or another act, and if the procedure is correctly followed. It must check if the limits of the powers given to the Union are respected, and if all provisions proposed are legally correct and respect legal principles, such as subsidiarity and proportionality. It must also check that a proper statement of reasons is provided in the recitals ('whereas' clauses) of the proposed act. These matters (legal basis, EU law, statement of reasons) constitute grounds for the possible annulment of a Council act by the Court of Justice of the EU.

In addition, the Legal Service often has to advise on the correct application of the Council's Rules of Procedure, for example, whether a quorum is met, whether the items on the provisional agenda have been included in good time, whether the Council session is to be re-transmitted to the public by television means, the possibility of adopting an act by a written procedure, rules on languages, publications in the Official Journal, etc.

The Legal Service also provides advice internally within the General Secretariat of the Council, on administrative and budgetary questions such as the application of the Financial Regulation, on the Staff Regulations, etc.

Last, but not least, the Legal Counsel was asked to act as the Legal Advisor to the Inter-Governmental Conferences which negotiated, drafted and agreed the Treaty of Maastricht (1991), of Amsterdam (1996) and of Nice (2000), the draft Constitution for Europe (2003) and the Treaty of Lisbon (2007).

3.1 THE EUROPEAN UNION

Opinions and written contributions of the Legal Service are produced as Council documents (in all twenty-three languages), and may not, unless there are exceptions, be disclosed.

Cases before the European courts

Litigation before the Court of Justice, the General Court and the Civil Service Tribunal accounts for, more or less, one-third of the workload of the Legal Advisors, although that proportion may differ largely from one to another. This task nearly always involves defending the Council against an action for the annulment of a Council act, a declaration of illegality or compensation for damages. Two, or sometimes three, members of the Legal Service are appointed by the Director-General to represent the Council in each case. They are usually the Legal Advisors responsible for the subject-area, and if necessary another one who is fluent in the language of the case.

In most cases, the Council wins the cases brought against it. If it loses, it must take the necessary measures to comply with the Court's judgment, e.g., by re-adopting an annulled act on another legal basis or after re-consulting the European Parliament, or by amending provisions which have been found contrary to the law.

Quality of the legislation

The Legal Service has an important role to play in improving the drafting quality of EU legislation, which must be as clear, simple and precise as possible for its users, whether they be national authorities, businesses or citizens generally. According to an Inter-Institutional Agreement signed by the European

Parliament, the Council and the Commission on 22 December 1998 on Common Guidelines for the quality of drafting of EU legislation,[10] the three institutions' legal services must put forward appropriate drafting suggestions with a view to making EU legislation clearer and more precise. The Council's Rules of Procedure[11] (Article 22) also stipulate that 'the Legal Service shall be responsible for checking the drafting quality of proposals and draft acts at the appropriate stage, as well as for bringing drafting suggestions to the attention of the Council and its bodies'.

This task is performed both by the Legal Advisors who follow proposals in the meetings of the Council and its preparatory bodies, as well as by the lawyers-linguist of the Directorate on Quality of Legislation. There are at least three lawyers-linguist for each of the twenty-three official languages of the Union. They are responsible for the final editing of all legal acts to be adopted by the Council. That involves laying the text out properly, using the right terminology and ensuring that all provisions have exactly the same meaning in all languages, as each of them is legally equally authentic.

3.2 Other international organisations

The organisation and tasks of the legal services of more classical intergovernmental organisations, among which the main ones are the following, have also been examined, in order to draw some comparative observations:

[10] *Official Journal of the EU*, C73, 17 March 1999.
[11] Council Decision 2009/937/EU of 1 December 2009; *Official Journal of the EU*, L325, 11 December 2009.

3.2 OTHER INTERNATIONAL ORGANISATIONS

- United Nations[12]
- World Trade Organization[13]
- International Monetary Fund[14]
- Council of Europe[15]
- Andean Community[16]
- Organization of American States[17]
- African Union[18]

3.2.1 Functions of a legal service in an international organisation

The following tasks are the usual ones given by international organisations to their legal services:

(3.2.1.1) Legal memory of the organisation

The legal service is often put in charge of the establishment and maintenance of the archives of the organisation. This includes not only exercising the task of depository of the treaties and agreements concluded by the organisation, or by its member states under its aegis (Council of Europe, Andean Pact, African Union, etc.), and of all the legal acts adopted within the organisation, but also sometimes the classification and

---

[12] See http://legal.un.org/ola/.
[13] See www.wto.org/english/thewto_e/secre_e/div_e.htm#legal.
[14] See www.imf.org/external/np/adm/rec/job/legal.htm.
[15] See www.coe.int under 'Directorate of Legal Advice and Public International Law (DLAPIL)'.
[16] See www.comunidadandina.org. See decisions 409 and 553.
[17] See www.oas.org/legal/intro.htm.
[18] See www.au.int/en/commission under 'Office of the Legal Counsel'.

identification of all documents, including the preparatory ones (Codification Division of the UN Legal Service), the indexation and computerisation of the archives, etc.

This also includes the publication of the legally binding legal acts, decisions, agreements or any other normative texts, either in an 'Official Journal' (like in the EU) or in Codes, or on a website. Organisations may choose to publish an official journal only on paper, or only in an electronic form, or both. Legally, the publication of a legal text will mark the date on which the text becomes legally binding for the member states, their administrations and possibly the economic operators and the consumers. Such a publication is therefore absolutely essential if and when a given organisation is trying to establish a single market among its member states. The legal services are often conferred the additional task of being the depository of international commitments taken by the organisation, and thus also being charge of publishing these commitments when they entail rights or obligations for third parties, including economic operators.

A choice an organisation has to make is to publish its texts either in one language only (European Free Trade Area, European Economic Area) or, if appropriate for practical or political reasons, in all official languages of its member states (EU), notwithstanding the cost and complexity it entails, or in a limited number of languages (UN, Council of Europe, OECD).

An option would also be to privatise some of these missions by outsourcing them, either to an agency or a firm in the private sector, or to the administration of one of the member states.

3.2 OTHER INTERNATIONAL ORGANISATIONS

(3.2.1.2) Legal adviser of the Secretariat

The usual and more logical way, which is followed in most international organisations, is to confer the task to be the legal adviser of the Secretariat on an in-house team of lawyers who are part of its legal service. However, the choice can be made to outsource this task to an external law firm, at least for some issues. The issues to be covered are to provide advice to the Secretary-General and the Secretariat of the organisation on legal aspects of administrative, budgetary and staff issues. This includes contracts for acquisition of buildings, goods and services and issues concerning privileges and immunities. Another option is to confer these tasks on another service of the Secretariat (for example, a department of the Directorate responsible for administrative and budgetary matters).

Therefore, one may choose between different options. However, the fact that these tasks have been conferred on their in-house legal service in most organisations (UN, EU, WTO, IMF, Council of Europe, Organization of American States, Andean Community, African Union) did not happen by chance. Legal problems – such as delicate issues of privileges and immunities – may relate to staff matters but may also concern the interpretation to be given to the constitutive texts of the organisation. Moreover, other tasks (for instance, on budgetary matters, or on contracts with third states, intergovernmental organisations or private firms) might be linked to substantive issues. This is why, given the imperative of coherence, the choice is often made to confer the totality of these tasks to the in-house legal service, it being understood that they should be dealt with by a specialised unit or directorate within that service.

As concerns legal advice to be given to the Secretary-General and to the Secretariat in their substantive (economic or political) tasks, such as in political-security matters and wherever the Secretary-General has to formulate suggestions to be addressed to the organisation decision-making bodies or/and to member states, the legal service may or may not (formally or informally) be involved, depending on the degree of 'integration' of the organisation concerned.

(3.2.1.3) Legal interpreter of normative texts, including the primary law of the organisation

In the most 'integrated' organisations, this task is often given to an independent Court of Justice (EU, Council of Europe, Andean Community). In most organisations, the Secretariat, with its legal service, plays a consultative role (UN, EU, WTO, Council of Europe, Organization of American States, Andean Community, African Union). No existing organisation gives to its legal service or Secretariat the power to give an obligatory interpretation.

There are organisations where the task of giving an authoritative interpretation of the founding Charter has been conferred on a Committee of a few member states (e.g., the North American Free Trade Area). One can imagine that this is not the wisest solution, as it may finish with a plenary Committee which would be unable to reach a solution through consensus. Some organisations have opted for a decision by a two-thirds majority on questions of interpretation (UN, WTO).

3.2 OTHER INTERNATIONAL ORGANISATIONS

(3.2.1.4) Giving legal assistance during the work of the organisation's organs as well as for the monitoring of the implementation of the organisation's decisions

In most organisations, the legal service gives its legal assistance to the organisation's bodies and to the Secretariat in fulfilling their tasks. It is sometimes also given the task of giving assistance to the surveillance systems, and more generally to any organ, mechanism or procedure aiming at monitoring the implementation of their legal obligations by the member states (WTO).

In a number of organisations, the legal service is tasked with helping the member states and their administrations to comply with the implementation of their commitments, in drafting legislation, etc. (IMF, EU Commission, Council of Europe).

(3.2.1.5) Giving legal assistance for the treatment of questions or informal complaints regarding the implementation of the organisation's decisions

Quite logically, the organisation's legal service, if in charge of helping with the interpretation of the organisation's legal texts and of giving legal assistance for the monitoring of their implementation by the member states, is also responsible for giving legal assistance to answer possible questions concerning those texts. Therefore, all questions (or informal complaints) received either from the member states or one of their public administrations or ministerial departments or agencies, or the economic operators or any other interested party on the correct implementation of a normative text of the organisation (whatever its legal form) is examined by the legal service, in order to help the Secretariat or the Presidency of the organisation to prepare an answer (EU).

From a legal point of view, this is all the more important for organisations that have the aim of establishing a genuine economic community. The reason for this necessity is that any differences in the interpretation of the legal texts to be implemented might entail distortions of competition between the economic operators or/and the member states, or entail differences of treatment between consumers/individuals according to the member states where they operate or consume, or be a negative incentive for potential investors to take the decisions to invest in this or that country.

(3.2.1.6) Giving legal assistance for the treatment of formal complaints regarding the implementation of the organisation's decisions

The role of the legal service in an organisation as regards formal complaints on the implementation of the organisation's decisions depends on the system in force for the legal settlement of disputes.

This role is natural when the Secretary-General of the organisation has been conferred the task of intervening during these procedures, to give her/his opinion about the scope of the organisation's texts at issue and about the interpretation to be given to them. Whatever the kind of organ, mechanism, procedure, court or tribunal which has been established with a view to settling disputes or examining infringements concerning the correct implementation of the organisation's texts, the

3.2 OTHER INTERNATIONAL ORGANISATIONS

legal assistance of the legal service is often considered as useful, and plays a major role, especially of course when this service is trusted as having demonstrated its neutrality and its good professional quality.

(3.2.1.7) Giving legal assistance for the representation of the organisation before a judicial organ

In cases when a court, tribunal, or any other kind of organ, with appropriate mechanisms or procedures, has been established and given the task of dealing with a dispute in which the organisation is interested or concerned, the organisation is generally represented by its Secretary-General. Sometimes, it is represented by its Presidency. In any case, whether the task is attributed to the organisation's Secretary-General or to its Presidency, the legal service plays a major role in helping the relevant institution fulfil its task in these legalistic matters.

However, there are different options between which the competent authorities of the organisation may choose. As this choice has to entail a complete trust from all member states, the task should be conferred on the most neutral and independent body. It goes without saying that in all intergovernmental organisations the Secretary-General and the legal service's actions are under the control of the competent ministerial bodies.

Another option is to have a standing list of lawyers or firms chosen by a board appointed by the decision-making body of the organisation, which offers choices to be made on a case-by-case basis. However, one should be aware of the necessity that those who are chosen must have a good knowledge of the organisation and of its political culture. Moreover, the need for continuity and coherence must not be forgotten.

3.2.2 Lessons drawn from the experiences of other international organisations

In the present state of intergovernmental organisations in the world, the most advanced and influential legal services are those of the institutions of the EU. Strong and neutral legal services exist also in other organisations, such as the United Nations or the International Monetary Fund. Actually, the strength of the legal service of an organisation depends on a number of factors.

(3.2.2.1) The rules and the modalities of the decision-making system

Rules establishing who makes decisions, and according to which procedure they are being made, are always the most delicate ones to establish in an intergovernmental organisation. While, in a classic international organisation, the rule of 'one state, one vote' generally applies, and either unanimity or two-thirds of the votes are necessary to decide (e.g., the General Assembly of the UN, or the intergovernmental conferences convened by the UN to adopt an international convention), this cannot be realistically the case in the most integrated organisations, such as the EU.

First, one has to take into account that, if one wants to be able to adopt decisions necessary to establish a customs union, a single market and an economic union, unanimity as a single and universal rule, without any exception, would be an impediment.

3.2 OTHER INTERNATIONAL ORGANISATIONS

Secondly, giving the same weighting vote to a state with a few hundreds of thousands of citizens/consumers as to another state with more than several millions of citizens/consumers would be neither equitable nor democratic. It would also entail the risk of adopting unrealistic decisions, which would be difficult to implement.

Therefore, the European Economic Community, then the European Community, now the European Union, has always taken into account the different sizes of the member states in the rules of decision-making. One of the major elements of the political and institutional architecture of the EU, as it has been painstakingly built up and finely tuned over the years, and to which the member states pay close attention, is the sharing and balance of powers. This concerns not only the share of powers between the different EU institutions, but also the respective weight given to each member state or to their nationals in the decision-taking system within each of those institutions. Member states are 'present' in the decision-taking system of each of the three political institutions of the EU. This is indirectly the case through the presence and the number of their nationals in the European Parliament and in the Commission. This is directly the case through the weight carried by the vote of the representative of their government in the Council.

An intergovernmental organisation must, in order to be able to take decisions, find a decision-taking system which avoids each decision having to be taken by common accord, unanimity or consensus of the member states. The question of how much weight should be given to each of the member states in the decision-making is of the utmost importance.

THE ASEAN LEGAL SERVICE

The different ways to adopt decisions
There are five different ways to decide in an institution or organ of an intergovernmental organisation. All of them are used in the European Council and in the EU Council, according to the importance and sensibility of the decisions to be taken:

- *Common agreement or common accord of the member states*: while common agreement was, and often still is, the 'normal' rule in classic international negotiations between states, in the EU this rule is applicable only when explicitly provided for in the Treaties. This rule symbolises the fact that, in certain areas, the system remains 'intergovernmental' in character, because each of the member states has to approve the decision explicitly (revision of the Treaties, choice of the seats of the institutions, languages, etc.).
- *Unanimity*: unanimity is equally applicable only when explicitly provided for in the Treaties. This rule means that a decision needs in principle a positive vote of all Members. Each member has a right of veto (negative vote). However, they may abstain and, in that case, the abstentions (whatever their number) do not prevent the adoption of decisions which require unanimity (see Articles 235(1) and 238(4) TFEU).
- *Consensus*: consensus is the normal rule for the European Council (see Article 15(4) TEU: 'Except where the Treaties provide otherwise, decisions of the European Council shall be taken by consensus'). This means that the decision is taken unless one or several members explicitly disagree. Silence or non-formal opposition is taken as acquiescence.
- *Qualified majority voting (QMV)*: QMV is the normal rule for the Council (see Article 16(3) TEU: 'The Council shall

3.2 OTHER INTERNATIONAL ORGANISATIONS

act by a qualified majority except where the Treaties provide otherwise'). QMV is submitted to sophisticated methods of calculation, the aim of which is to get a difficult and delicate balance between the principle that any member state, whatever its population and wealth, has to get a say in the decision-making, and the principle of taking into account the relative importance of each state, therefore a balance between the principle of classic diplomacy of the equality of states ('one state, one vote') and the principle of reality and of democracy ('one man, one vote').

- *Simple majority*: simple majority is applicable both in the European Council and in the Council only when explicitly provided for by the Treaties, which is mainly the case for the adoption of decisions on procedure, including the adoption of the Rules of Procedure of both institutions.[19]

One has to add that the European Parliament has now, through successive amendments of the EU Treaties, been conferred important powers of co-decision with the Council. For the adoption of legislative acts, and unless the Treaties provide otherwise, it is not only necessary to obtain a qualified majority of the votes in the Council but also a majority in a vote taken in the European Parliament. For some important decisions, the Treaties provide that a majority of the Members of the

---

[19] For a list of cases where unanimity, common accord or consensus continues to apply after the entry into force of the Lisbon Treaty, see Appendix 8 of Jean-Claude Piris, *The Lisbon Treaty – A Legal and Political Analysis* (Cambridge University Press, Cambridge, 2010), pp. 386–97.

European Parliament (and not only a majority of the votes of those present and voting) is necessary for a decision to be taken.

(3.2.2.2) The modalities for monitoring the implementation by the member states of the decisions taken by the competent organs of the organisation

These modalities may be:

- internal and not obligatory (recommendations made by an internal organ or institution),
- internal and obligatory (legally binding decision of a court, tribunal or panel specific to the organisation),
- external and not obligatory or
- external and obligatory.

(3.2.2.3) The modalities for the settlement of disputes concerning the implementation of the decisions taken by the competent organs of the organisation

These modalities may provide for:

- legally binding or not legally binding procedures, resulting in
- legally binding or not legally binding decisions, taken either by
- political organs or judicial organs, those organs being established
- on a permanent or an ad hoc basis.

In an international organisation:

1. where there is no legally binding procedure similar to an infringement procedure, and

2. where there is no court or tribunal, and no preliminary rulings requested by national courts in order to attain a great degree of uniformity in the interpretation of the applicable law

the necessity of, at least, having a high quality legal service is of the utmost importance.

According to the authors of this book, this is a minimum without which the hope of building an economic union and a single market should be abandoned.

3.3 Functions of an ASEAN Legal Service

What are the lessons to be drawn from Sections 1 and 2?

On one side, as Section 1 has demonstrated, ASEAN cannot be equipped with similar institutions and rules as those of the EU: some of its characteristics are not comparable with those of the EU. They are more similar to those of classic intergovernmental international organisations, governed by classic public international law.

However, on the other side, the aims of ASEAN have now been modified by the Charter. It must not be seen any more as similar in nature to most of these international organisations, as it has been shown in Section 2. ASEAN has now been tasked by its member states to establish an economic community and a single market.

According to the authors of this book, this implies a degree of integration superior to most existing intergovernmental international organisations: in order for an economic community and a single market to work, investors and economic operators have to be assured that all their competitors will play on the same level playing field and will be bound by and obey the same rules.

The issue is therefore to try and suggest the establishment in ASEAN of a legal service that:

1. in the present circumstances, could be politically suited to ASEAN, with its current characteristics, and help it to function properly;
2. in the short and medium terms, could help ASEAN to fulfil as much as possible the hopes created by the ASEAN Charter, especially in the establishment of an economic community and a single market; and
3. as to the future, would be able to adapt to possible evolutions of ASEAN.

Starting from that point of departure, what are the most pressing needs in order to build an economic community and an internal market?

On the one hand, ASEAN competent authorities will have to adopt decisions which would be legally properly drafted, sufficiently precise and unambiguous.

On the other hand, ASEAN authorities might wish to have, in the future, a service with the potential such as to be able to deliver non-obligatory and neutral views in case of a non-application or of an incorrect application by a member state of the decisions made by ASEAN.

The conviction of the authors is that the best solution would be to establish an independent and professional legal service, which could, inter alia:

3.3 FUNCTIONS OF AN ASEAN LEGAL SERVICE

(a) in the short term, help draft in a professional way decisions to be adopted by the competent organs of the organisation, and

(b) in the future, help, in the absence of any court or tribunal, to try to establish, in case of disputes on the application of those decisions, a kind of a non-obligatory procedure in which it could play a role.

The authors recognise that this would be an imperfect and minimal way to try to allow ASEAN to implement the Charter.

However, taking into account both the history and the psychology of ASEAN as well as of its member states' authorities, they think that it is the only realistic way and that it would nevertheless be useful, certainly in a first stage, and possibly later, in view of a future possible evolution of ASEAN.

3.3.1 *The necessity for a separate Legal Service*

The creation of a Legal Division to 'support the implementation of the ASEAN Charter' is already envisaged in the ASEAN Political-Security Community Blueprint.[20] In Bali Concord III it was declared that there should be an enhanced ASEAN Secretariat with the capacity to 'provide effective support in projecting ASEAN's collective undertakings at the global level'.[21] It is suggested that the establishment of a

---

[20] This forms part of the Roadmap for the ASEAN Community (2009–15). See para. A.2.1(iii).

[21] 2011 Bali Declaration on ASEAN Community in a Global Community of Nations (Bali Concord III), penultimate para.

fully fledged legal service as part of the infrastructure of the ASEAN Community is essential to the achievement of the aims of the Charter and Bali Concord III. There are three cardinal advantages to the creation of an independent ASEAN Legal Service: expertise, experience and neutrality.

Up to now, legal expertise has resided in the national delegations to ASEAN meetings. The Secretariat is seldom, if ever, in a position to provide legal advice to delegations. During the drafting of the Charter, there was no legal adviser from the Secretariat. That role was played by Secretary-General Ong Keng Yong, who was trained as a lawyer. This was entirely serendipitous, as there is no requirement that the Secretary-General or DSGs be legally trained. One cannot count on it in future; and, in any case, the Secretary-General and DSGs do not attend every ASEAN meeting. The lawyers attached to national delegations seldom have any real expertise in ASEAN matters, being for the most part assigned for a project or meeting. As was pointed out to one of the authors by senior ASEAN officials, most national delegations are staffed by persons who do not specialise in ASEAN affairs or who only attend a particular meeting on an annual basis. In effect, they are part-timers where ASEAN is concerned. If ASEAN is to evolve properly into a rules-based organisation as envisaged it is imperative to develop a core of legally trained persons with expertise in the rules, regulations, treaties and agreements that apply. National delegations cannot be counted on to supply this expertise. Only a central service can do so.

Following on from the previous point, there is no guarantee that lawyers from the member states will have sufficient experience in ASEAN matters. The experience in

3.3 FUNCTIONS OF AN ASEAN LEGAL SERVICE

Singapore of one of the authors was that legal officers do not remain assigned to ASEAN matters for extended periods. There is a relatively quick turnover as officers are posted to other branches of the home legal service; indeed, the best officers are likely to move on to other things in relatively short order. It would be surprising if this were not the case with other ASEAN member states. For ASEAN to evolve properly into a law-abiding community as envisaged, it is necessary to have an experienced corps of lawyers who are familiar with ASEAN affairs over the years and who know the background to the various ASEAN initiatives. Again, it is too much to expect that national delegations will be able to assign legal officers for the long term. Only a proper ASEAN Legal Service can do this.

Finally, and possibly most importantly, an ASEAN Legal Service will be impartial. The dynamic within ASEAN remains competitive despite the desire to cooperate. This will be the case for the foreseeable future. National delegations have national positions to defend; these may not be consistent with the overall interests of ASEAN as a separate entity. Lawyers attached to national delegations are constrained by their instructions; they cannot abandon national negotiating positions in the wider interest of ASEAN as an organisation. For this reason, it will be difficult for a national delegation to defer to another on legal matters. The Charter-drafting process illustrates this. At the first meeting of the High Level Task Force (HLTF) for the Drafting of the ASEAN Charter it was proposed that the task of producing a draft be divided up among the delegations. This was not agreed to. The result was that there were several drafts presented by different delegations. Much time was spent reconciling the different drafts. It would have been so much more logical and efficient if a single draft prepared by a neutral party had been presented for consideration by the delegations. That neutral role can only be played by a separate ASEAN Legal Service, independent of national bias.

In Chapter 1 we traced the development of ASEAN and its characteristics as an organisation. The first part of Chapter 2 explains the current reality. The immediate goal of ASEAN is to create an ASEAN community by 2015, anchored on the ASEAN Economic Community. The ultimate goal, according to the EPG, is an ASEAN Union – which realistically would probably take the form of a confederation of some sort rather than a federation. Though it is hard at the present moment to envisage a time when ASEAN will reach that level of integration it should be recalled that the idea of a Charter was first mooted in 1974.[22] The suggestion was made by the Filipino Foreign Secretary Mr Carlos Romulo. Thirty-three years passed before the Charter became a reality. The founders of ASEAN would be astounded by the level of integration that the association has reached today. The suggestion for an ASEAN Union was also the suggestion of a Filipino, Mr Fidel Ramos. It was in the Report of the Eminent Persons' Group. The Report of the Eminent Persons' Group was accepted by the leaders at the Twelfth Summit. Big ideas have a long gestation period. One should not be so ready to dismiss the idea of a Union out of hand, despite the fact that it appears to have

---

[22] Joint Communiqué of the Seventh AMM (Jakarta, May 1974), para. 9.

3.3 FUNCTIONS OF AN ASEAN LEGAL SERVICE

been quietly shelved.[23] The deadline for the establishment of an ASEAN Union is indeterminate; but, until the leaders formally abandon this aspiration, ASEAN should be progressing towards the formation of a union. With the past, the present and the future in mind, we can set out the functions of the ASEAN Legal Service.

3.3.2 Functions of the Legal Service

It is tempting to look for a 'model' on which to base an ASEAN Legal Service. There are many other intergovernmental organisations which might provide such a model, in particular the EU. The temptation should be firmly resisted. No two intergovernmental organisations are identical. The way that such an organisation works in practice is a function of its history and the culture of its members. Nevertheless, a survey of other organisations is instructive. One may distil several principles of general application.

To summarise, an ASEAN Legal Service would have a significant role to play in the development of ASEAN as a rules-based, law-abiding organisation, in the following areas:

- drafting of agreements, rules and regulations for internal as well as external purposes;
- providing the institutional legal memory of ASEAN by maintaining records, updating agreements and other legal instruments, and ensuring that inconsistencies are resolved;

---

[23] In drafting the Charter, instructions were given by the Foreign Ministers to avoid mentioning an ASEAN Union for the time being.

- providing impartial expert legal advice to the ASEAN Summit, the member states, the Secretary-General, the Community Councils, the ministerial bodies and the Committee of Permanent Representatives, as well as other ASEAN bodies;
- assisting the Secretary-General in monitoring the implementation of and compliance with ASEAN agreements;
- providing legal representation for ASEAN as an entity; and
- assisting the ASEAN Summit, the Secretary-General and other dispute resolution bodies in the settlement of disputes.

(3.3.2.1) Drafting of agreements

ASEAN aims to be a rules-based organisation. Such an organisation needs clear rules. There are four aspects to this: first, the internal agreements that bind ASEAN member states and create the infrastructure of the organisation; secondly, the agreements between ASEAN and outside parties; thirdly, the internal rules and regulations necessary to realise the ASEAN single market and production base; and, fourthly, the harmonisation of the domestic laws of ASEAN member states. The first and second aspects are self-explanatory. The third and fourth aspects are new. They arise because of the commitment in the Community Blueprints[24] to create a regional system of rules and regulations and to harmonise the laws of member states in order to realise the ASEAN Community by 2015.

---

[24] Annexed to the Cha-Am Hua Hin Declaration of 2009 as the Roadmap for the ASEAN Community (2009–15). The Declaration was issued at the Fourteenth ASEAN Summit.

3.3 FUNCTIONS OF AN ASEAN LEGAL SERVICE

Thus, for instance, the main focus in the creation of the single market and production base will be the elimination of non-tariff barriers; regional rules consistent with international best practices are required.[25] Customs procedures and formalities are to be harmonised in accordance with international standards.[26] A comprehensive agreement to protect investors is to be implemented.[27] There is to be harmonisation of, inter alia, capital market standards for offerings of debt securities and disclosure requirements,[28] the regulatory framework for agricultural products derived from biotechnology,[29] and the legal infrastructure for electronic contracting and dispute resolution.[30] The Economic Community Blueprint also envisages ASEAN-wide efforts to promote competition policy, enhance intellectual property rights, develop information technology infrastructure and liberalise transport. In the Socio-Economic Community Blueprint there is a commitment to harmonise national food safety regulations in accordance with international standards.[31] All of these will require detailed rules and regulations. The Socio-Economic Community Blueprint also envisages that member states will work towards an ASEAN instrument on the protection and promotion of the rights of migrant workers.[32] There is to be cooperation on protection of the environment, sustainable use of resources and regulation of

---

[25] ASEAN Economic Community Blueprint, para. 14(v).
[26] Ibid., para. 17(i).   [27] Ibid., para. 27.   [28] Ibid., para. 31.
[29] Ibid., para. 38(vi).   [30] Ibid., para. 59(ii).   [31] Ibid., para. 21(i).
[32] Ibid., para. 28(i). Progress on this is slow. See the Chairman's Statement of the Twenty-first ASEAN Summit (Phnom Penh, November 2012) para. 56.

the transport of hazardous waste, amongst other things. As far as the Political-Security Community is concerned, ASEAN member states pledge to cooperate in combating the trade in illegal drugs, transnational crimes, people trafficking, cybercrimes and terrorism. At some point, regional treaties on all these matters will be necessary.

The present mode of making agreements is ad hoc. It depends exclusively on member states as the ASEAN Secretariat does not have the resources. Several problems arise from this. Some of the member states also suffer from resource constraints when it comes to legal drafting and research. There may be turf battles between ministries that impinge on the draft that is put up for consideration. Most importantly, there is always the possibility that any draft will be influenced consciously or unconsciously by the interests of the country entrusted with the drafting. This situation may be tolerable for agreements of the first sort, viz., those among ASEAN states themselves. The draft will be picked over in negotiations and knocked into a form acceptable to all. It is less acceptable when the agreement is between ASEAN and an external party. Each member state will look out for its own interests, but the interests of ASEAN as a whole are not taken care of. When it comes to harmonisation of domestic laws and the creation of regional rules, as the ASEAN Community Roadmap requires, this clearly cannot be left exclusively to the member states themselves. A neutral party at the centre is necessary to provide coordination, expertise and objectivity.

A rules-based organisation whose working language is English must have a core of competent legal draughtsmen. These experts will be entrusted with the task of 'scrubbing' the

3.3 FUNCTIONS OF AN ASEAN LEGAL SERVICE

text of the many documents that emanate from ASEAN meetings, rather than leaving that role to the national delegations. Apart from the issue of linguistic and legal competence, there is also the matter of political neutrality. A non-English-speaking delegation may well feel disadvantaged when confronted with another national delegation which is comfortable working in English, especially when dealing with legal documents which impose obligations on member states. Having the politically neutral members of the ASEAN Legal Service scrub the text should allay any suspicions of bias in the language of such documents.

Most importantly, an ASEAN Legal Service will be able to provide dedicated and continuous attention to the drafting of agreements. At present, the member states do not have lawyers whose exclusive concern is ASEAN. This inhibits the development of expertise. Experience in ASEAN affairs is essential for good drafting. This experience can only be accumulated if there is a proper legal service.

(3.3.2.2) Institutional memory and avoidance of inconsistencies

The Charter sets out various organs in Chapter IV. To recapitulate, at the top of the hierarchy is the aptly named ASEAN Summit, which is the supreme policy-making organ of ASEAN.[33] This comprises the heads of government and executive heads of state of the ASEAN member states. Below the Summit is the ASEAN Coordinating Council (ACC), consisting of the Foreign Ministers.[34] The ACC prepares the Summit

---

[33] ASEAN Charter, Article 7.   [34] Ibid., Article 8.

meetings and (in theory) coordinates the activities of the ASEAN Political-Security Community Council, the ASEAN Economic Community Council and the ASEAN Socio-Cultural Community Council.[35] The Community Councils have general oversight of the sectoral ministerial bodies.[36] Below the sectoral ministerial bodies are various senior officials' meetings, which prepare the meetings of the ministers.

Politically, it is necessary for each of these bodies to have 'deliverables' at the end of their meetings, i.e., tangible proof that something has been done by them. These deliverables almost invariably involve the issuance of a declaration or adoption of some sort of agreement. The volume of documents can only increase with the increased tempo of sectoral meetings.[37] The three pillars of the ASEAN Community function practically independently of one another.[38] It is inevitable that sooner or later there will be clashes between what one sectoral body has agreed and existing obligations adopted by another sectoral body. Without a

---

[35] Ibid., Article 9.
[36] Ibid., Article 10. The list of such ministerial bodies is to be found in Annex 1 to the Charter. There are six under the Political-Security Community Council, fourteen under the Economic Community Council and seventeen under the Socio-Cultural Community Council, for a grand total of thirty-seven.
[37] At the time of writing, the Secretary-General has estimated that there are more than 1,200 ASEAN meetings a year.
[38] In conversation with one of the authors, ASEAN officials and Permanent Representatives confirmed that the Committee of Permanent Representatives (CPR) deals almost exclusively with matters pertaining to the Political-Security Community. In theory, the CPR should be coordinating across the three pillars to assist the ACC.

3.3 FUNCTIONS OF AN ASEAN LEGAL SERVICE

central authority having oversight, there will be a real risk of inconsistencies and even outright contradictions in the noodle-bowl of obligations undertaken by member states. As discussed in the previous section, the member states do not have legal experts permanently dedicated to ASEAN affairs. The necessary expertise and experience can only be developed by a proper professional legal service that deals exclusively with ASEAN matters.

It is also imperative that some department should be responsible for monitoring the many agreements that emanate from the various meetings to at least highlight inconsistencies before they become embarrassingly obvious when there is an open clash. The task of keeping track of these agreements and updating them as they are amended is also crucial. A rules-based organisation can only thrive if the rules can be found. There has to be an authoritative source for ASEAN agreements, rules and regulations.[39] The ASEAN Legal Service should fulfil this essential task.

(3.3.2.3) **Giving legal advice**

One of the primary roles of any legal service is the giving of advice. In the ASEAN context the need for a legal unit to render such advice in economic matters was recognised nearly a decade ago. The High Level Task Force (HLTF) on Economic Integration recommended in its report that a legal unit be established to give advice to member states on trade

---

[39] In the absence of such a source, the Centre for International Law, National University of Singapore maintains an ASEAN documents database on its website: cil.nus.edu.sg.

157

disputes.[40] The advice of the legal unit is not binding, i.e., non-authoritative. Member states are free to ignore it, though no doubt the fact that such advice was given and ignored would be a factor taken into consideration if the matter goes to dispute resolution. The Charter envisages that the Secretariat will have a limited advisory role in interpretation of its provisions.[41] Rules of procedure for this have been prepared by the Committee of Permanent Representatives. Noteworthy is the constraint placed on the Secretariat. Rule 2(1) provides: 'The interpretation of the ASEAN Charter by the ASEAN Secretariat shall be non-binding and non-authoritative in nature and shall not be considered as representing the view of any member state or of ASEAN as an intergovernmental organisation.' This practically deprives the Secretariat's advice of any value and reflects a distressing lack of faith in the central ASEAN institution.

If ASEAN is to be taken seriously as a rules-based organisation, this aversion to accepting authoritative advice from a neutral party must be overcome. Member states must get used to hearing things that they do not want to hear when it comes to legal matters. The most appropriate body to render such advice would be an independent legal service uninfluenced by national agendas.

However, it is not only member states that require advice and it is not only in the realm of trade that disputes

---

[40] See para. 14(v) of the HLTF's recommendations, which were annexed to the Declaration of ASEAN Concord II, issued at the Ninth ASEAN Summit (October 2003).
[41] ASEAN Charter, Article 51.

3.3 FUNCTIONS OF AN ASEAN LEGAL SERVICE

will arise. In its advisory capacity, the Legal Service will probably find its hands full. Member states may ask for interpretations not only of the Charter but also of other ASEAN instruments. There is a similar need on the part of the Community Councils and multifarious ministerial bodies. This is particularly the case where the ASEAN Economic Community is concerned, since economic integration requires the existence of a coherent and enforceable set of rules and regulations. Bodies like the AEM, the ASEAN Investment Area Council (AIA Council) and the Senior Economic Officials' Meeting (SEOM) are the key to the creation of a viable single market and production base. These bodies need to have access to impartial and credible legal advice in the discharge of their functions.

The Secretary-General requires strong legal backup to discharge the many tasks that he is entrusted with. ASEC will also need legal advice in order to function efficiently, not least in its relations with the host country. To give an example, it is impossible to negotiate leases and contracts for services without competent legal advice; to attempt this without the input of legal professionals is courting trouble. Finally, the Committee of Permanent Representatives sorely requires the assistance of a dedicated corps of lawyers to ease their load. When concluding a host country agreement, for instance, who represents the interests of ASEAN as a whole now that the organisation has a separate legal personality? The only logical candidate would be an ASEAN Legal Service.

The legal services of the member states cannot fulfil the need for legal advice even if officers could be assigned on a long-term basis. There will always be the suspicion of national bias, whether conscious or unconscious. A neutral ASEAN service is required if legal advice is to be credible and authoritative.

(3.3.2.4) Monitoring implementation of and compliance with ASEAN agreements

One major criticism of ASEAN, voiced among others by former Secretaries-General,[42] is that implementation of agreements is very patchy (to put it diplomatically). It is difficult to avoid the impression that for some member states in the Chair, having a major agreement or declaration or action plan adopted during their term is the important thing; whether or not there is any follow-through is secondary. This was one of the major flaws in the system that the EPG recognised as requiring urgent attention. The EPG recommended that the Secretary-General be entrusted with the task of monitoring compliance with ASEAN agreements.[43] The Charter now provides that one of the Secretary-General's functions is to facilitate and monitor progress in the implementation of ASEAN agreements and decisions, and submit an annual report on the work of ASEAN to the ASEAN Summit'.[44] The Secretary-General is also to 'monitor the compliance with the findings, recommendations or decisions resulting from an ASEAN dispute settlement mechanism, and submit a report to the ASEAN Summit'.[45] These two provisions taken together

---

[42] See para. 44 of the Report of the Eminent Persons' Group on the ASEAN Charter. The same point was repeated to one of the authors in conversation with former Secretaries-General.
[43] Ibid., para. 45.   [44] ASEAN Charter, Article 11(2)(b).
[45] Ibid., Article 27(1).

3.3 FUNCTIONS OF AN ASEAN LEGAL SERVICE

give effect to the EPG's recommendation. As discussed in the previous chapters, the monitoring role of the Secretary-General has expanded considerably over the years. He is now responsible for monitoring the implementation of the Roadmap for the ASEAN Community as well as mobilising the resources from member states and external parties to realise this.[46]

The logical course would be for the Secretary-General to be assisted by legally trained officers in monitoring compliance by member states with the rules. This monitoring function is complementary to the task of maintaining the Table of Ratifications. In the course of keeping the Table of Ratifications up to date, it will become clear whether or not an agreement is on track for implementation. It will then be up to the ASEAN Summit to decide what is to be done. This will be a political rather than a legal decision.

Thinking further ahead, there is at present no mechanism for the Secretary-General to initiate action to secure compliance by a member state with its obligations, beyond reporting the matter to the ASEAN Summit for a political decision. However, if ASEAN is to be taken seriously as a rules-based organisation, some such mechanism needs to be introduced in future. 'Naming and shaming' may be more consistent with the ASEAN way,[47] but a rules-based organisation needs legal teeth to enforce compliance with legal obligations. The Charter puts the onus of enforcement on a member state that is affected by non-compliance when a dispute

---

[46] Cha-Am Hua Hin Declaration on the Roadmap for the ASEAN Community (2009–15), paras. 4 and 5.
[47] Or, more precisely up to now, not naming and not shaming.

settlement mechanism has been invoked.[48] There is a political cost involved in invocation of dispute settlement mechanisms. Such factors as the desire to preserve bilateral goodwill or the need to avoid complicating a difficult bilateral relationship may inhibit a member state from insisting on compliance by another member state. There is no explicit provision for anyone else to complain when member states neglect to implement agreements. For the single market and production base to work efficiently, the Secretary-General (or some other authority, yet to be established) needs the power to compel compliance if no member state will take on the task. Politically, it would be easier for a neutral institution to initiate compliance proceedings rather than leave it to the member states. If this task is to be entrusted to the Secretary-General, he needs a strong legal backup team that can only be provided by a proper legal service.

(3.3.2.5) Legal representation

ASEAN now has a legal personality separate from the member states.[49] The intent of Article 3 of the Charter is to create a juridical person that can own property[50] and enforce rights independently of the member states. The member states are obliged to give effect to this by domestic legislation.[51]

---

[48] ASEAN Charter, Article 27(2).   [49] Ibid., Article 3.
[50] See, e.g., ASEAN Charter, Article 55 which vests the assets and funds of the organisation hitherto held by the Secretariat or other bodies in ASEAN as a distinct entity.
[51] See ASEAN Charter, Article 5(2). In the Singapore Declaration on the ASEAN Charter (issued at the Thirteenth ASEAN Summit in November 2007), the leaders reiterated the commitment of each member state to undertake all appropriate measures to implement the Charter.

3.3 FUNCTIONS OF AN ASEAN LEGAL SERVICE

Inevitably, ASEAN will become embroiled in legal disputes, whether involving commercial contracts, tenancies or employment matters. No doubt legal counsel will be instructed to appear in domestic forums to deal with these matters. The instructions, however, should come from persons well versed in legal matters, the equivalent of in-house counsel in a commercial organisation. This will ensure that ASEAN's interests are properly protected. It may even be necessary on occasion for ASEAN legal officers to appear before small claims tribunals, employment arbitration bodies or other legal forums to represent the organisation. It would be unwise to entrust such tasks to officials who have no legal training at all; this would be a recipe for confusion. Representing ASEAN before legal tribunals would be a natural role for an ASEAN Legal Service.

(3.3.2.6) Settlement of disputes

At the moment, the dispute settlement mechanisms under the Charter do not envisage the intervention of the Secretary-General or ASEC except to monitor the implementation of decisions.[52] However, even here there is scope for the assistance of a legal service. It is impossible for the Secretary-General personally to supervise compliance with decisions reached by an ASEAN dispute settlement mechanism. That task would have to be delegated to some other body. While it is possible to entrust non-lawyers with such a role, it would be more expedient that legally trained persons do this. If there is any question as to what exactly the decision is or as to its precise legal effects, any non-legal department would be

---

[52] See ASEAN Charter, Article 27(1).

forced to refer the matter to the lawyers; better to cut out one step in the process and have the legal service monitor compliance from the start.

Going beyond the rather modest role that the member states have conferred on the Secretary-General and ASEC, it should be recalled that the Report of the Eminent Persons' Group envisaged that the Secretary-General should be a personage of significant standing with the status of a minister. To treat him merely as an amanuensis would be a total waste. When drafting the Charter it was intended that the Secretary-General would have a role in dispute settlement, by providing good offices, mediation or conciliation.[53] A similar role for the Secretary-General is provided for in the Vientiane Protocol.[54] In fulfilling such a role the Secretary-General would have to be supported by a dedicated corps of experienced lawyers and not have to depend on ad hoc legal advice furnished by the member states.

The Preah Vihear case discussed in Chapter 2 vividly illustrates the constraints on the Secretary-General. The incumbent Secretary-General was marginalised because he had been a minister in one of the disputing countries, viz., Thailand. Fortunately, the Chair of ASEAN was held by Indonesia and Foreign Minister Natalegawa was an experienced diplomat. ASEAN cannot count on such serendipitous circumstances when disputes between member states arise in future. The principal problem is that the Secretary-General is nominated

---

[53] Ibid., Article 23(2). The Protocol to the ASEAN Charter on Dispute Settlement Mechanisms 2010 now formalises the procedure.
[54] Protocol on Enhanced Dispute Settlement Mechanism 2004, Article 4(3).

3.3 FUNCTIONS OF AN ASEAN LEGAL SERVICE

by the member states in alphabetical rotation. While the Charter provides that the Secretary-General should not receive instructions from any government,[55] it is natural and inevitable that parties to a dispute may not have implicit faith in a Secretary-General who is a national of one of the disputants. The solution, it is suggested, is for the Secretary-General to appoint a neutral special envoy to provide good offices, conciliation or mediation. This would take care of the problem of bias. Such an envoy would need just as much legal support as the Secretary-General himself. No member state could provide this – it has to come from a neutral ASEAN institution. The logical candidate would be an ASEAN Legal Service.

The ASEAN Summit also has a significant role to play in dispute settlement. Where disputes remain unresolved[56] or where there has been non-compliance with the decision of a dispute settlement body[57] the matter will be referred to the Summit for decision. It is inconceivable that the leaders will personally consider the matter; in the time-honoured way, they will task some other body to make a report to them. It is undesirable for an organisation that aspires to be rules-based for such decisions to be made on political grounds alone. If ASEAN is to develop properly, the appeal to the Summit should be treated like an appeal to a final appellate body. It is suggested that the logical course would be to entrust the matter to a neutral person or body, supported by an ASEAN Legal Service. No other practical

---

[55] ASEAN Charter, Article 11(8)(b).   [56] Ibid., Article 26.
[57] Ibid., Article 27(2).

alternative suggests itself if the ASEAN dispute settlement mechanisms are to achieve credibility.

Finally, a look into the future. For investor–state disputes, the High Level Task Force on ASEAN Economic Integration also recommended the creation of the ASEAN Consultation to Solve Trade and Investment Issues (ACT).[58] This is a network of government agencies, one from each member state, which allows a private investor to 'cut through red tape and achieve speedy resolution of operational problems encountered'. The complainant can request his country's ACT to direct the problem to the proper domestic agency or another country's ACT if there is a cross-border dispute. If the cross-border dispute is not resolved, the complainant may request his government to raise the matter under a dispute settlement mechanism. At some point it may be desirable for some central ASEAN body to filter such complaints and determine whether there is indeed ground for the invocation of the Vientiane Protocol or other dispute settlement mechanism. The 2009 ASEAN Comprehensive Investment Agreement (ACIA) preserves the application of the Vientiane Protocol where there is an investment dispute between member states.[59]

---

[58] See Annex 1 of the HLTF Report, which was incorporated into Bali Concord II (October 2003). The ACT can be accessed through the ASEAN website: www.asean.org.
[59] 2009 ASEAN Comprehensive Investment Agreement (ACIA), Article 27. The ACIA has detailed provisions on settlement of investor–state disputes, which include the possibility of arbitration; see ACIA Section B, Articles 28–41. It is now in force: see Press Release dated 4 April 2012 issued after the Twentieth ASEAN Summit in Phnom Penh.

3.4 STRUCTURE OF AN ASEAN LEGAL SERVICE

There are also ambitious plans in the Roadmap for the ASEAN Community (2009–15) for the creation of various commissions. For instance, ASEAN is to work towards a commission for the protection of the rights of women and children[60] and an ASEAN instrument on the promotion and protection of the rights of migrant workers.[61] The ASEAN Intergovernmental Commission on Human Rights (AICHR) has finished the ASEAN Human Rights Declaration.[62] It is not beyond the realm of possibility that mechanisms may be established to deal with complaints by individuals and organisations regarding a breach of their rights. It would be natural to entrust an ASEAN Legal Service with the task of filtering these complaints before they are referred to the appropriate dispute resolution bodies.

3.4 Structure of an ASEAN Legal Service

In order to interpret and help implement the Charter and the Blueprint, all ASEAN organs need the establishment of a sound legal service, competent, specialised and impartial, of the highest professional quality, which could be trusted by the

---

[60] Blueprint on the ASEAN Socio-Cultural Community 2009, para. 27(i). This is now in operation. It was reported at the Twenty-first ASEAN Summit (Phnom Penh, November 2012) that the Commission was finalising its five-year work plan for 2012–16.
[61] Blueprint on the ASEAN Socio-Cultural Community 2009, para. 28(i). This is crawling along slowly. See the Chairman's Statement of the Twenty-first ASEAN Summit (Phnom Penh, November 2012) para. 56.
[62] Adopted at the Twenty-first ASEAN Summit (Phnom Penh, November 2012).

ten member states with their own different laws, legal procedures and legal cultures and histories. This trust is indispensable to help to try and find solutions, at any stage, which should be founded on the rule of law and not on political preferences or economic interests. Such a trust may be ensured if the Head of the Legal Service and his/her deputies, as well as the other members of the Legal Service, are of the highest professional quality, independent, chosen according to their merits and wisdom, and having an indisputable legal authority. If these conditions are met, the Legal Service will bring a real added value to the assistance given by the Secretariat.

3.4.1 *The choice of a single Legal Service*

Taking into account the history of ASEAN, the essential characteristics of its institutional architecture, and especially its decision-making process, the choice between several legal services and a single one has to be made.

On the one hand, there is no equivalent of a Commission, like in the EU, on which ASEAN would have conferred both the exclusive task of preparation and of initiative of most legal acts of the organisation and the task of monitoring their correct implementation by the member states. This was the essential reason why the Commission needed a legal service distinct from the Legal Service(s) of the EU legislator (initially, only the EU Council of Ministers, later, both the Council and the European Parliament).

On the other hand, another possible option would be to establish different legal services taking into account the ASEAN architecture. Thus, one legal service could be

3.4 STRUCTURE OF AN ASEAN LEGAL SERVICE

established for each level of the ASEAN organ concerned: a first one for the Summit, a second one for the ministerial bodies, and a third one for the senior officials' meetings. However, such an option would not be advisable, as it would entail risks of legal disagreements between these different legal services, apart from the waste of resources through duplication.

Another option would be that each of the three ASEAN Community Councils would each have its own Legal Service. The first one would be more specialised in foreign policy, defence and transnational crime. The second one would concentrate on economic and financial matters, including agriculture, transport and energy. The third one would be specialised in culture, education, environment, social policy, etc., according to Annex 1 of the ASEAN Charter. This option would have the advantage of having specialised legal services. However, it would also have the disadvantage of not having a single body with horizontal/institutional knowledge, able to help preserve the coherence of all decisions prepared by the Community Councils. It is true that a good legal service should have competent lawyers in all these fields. Therefore, this is something one will have to keep in mind when designing the composition of the future ASEAN Legal Service.

Multiple legal services are not a practical option. First, there would be duplication and waste of scarce resources. Even the best-funded organisation cannot justify overlapping jobs to this extent. Secondly, it will be difficult enough to find sufficient competent staff for a single legal service. Staffing multiple services would be out of the question. Thirdly, and most importantly, it is essential that the Legal Service should have a broad view of all areas of ASEAN activity. Splitting the service risks creating narrow silos without contact with one another. Coordination among the three pillars leaves much to be desired. The impetus should be towards unification rather than division. Thus, it is clear that the only real option is the creation of a single unified Legal Service for all three pillars, serving all the organs.

The issue of whether the Legal Service should be part of the Secretariat is another matter to be decided. It may be that a separate EU Commission-type institution may be necessary in future, or that the Secretary-General's office may evolve into something more substantial. However, at present, the only viable host for the Legal Service would be the ASEAN Secretariat. It would be undesirable to set up a free-standing Legal Service independent of the Secretariat, as this would involve the creation of a separate administrative structure.

3.4.2 Essential characteristics of the Legal Service

It is quite difficult for any sovereign nation state to accept the sharing of a part of its sovereignty with others, in order to build with them a single market and an economic community. It will be especially the case for the ten member states of ASEAN, which are quite heterogeneous, be it in geographical, demographic, economic, cultural or political terms and which have their own history, very different from each other, and their own political culture.

In order to be successful in implementing the Charter, the ASEAN countries will absolutely need strong common

3.4 STRUCTURE OF AN ASEAN LEGAL SERVICE

institutions, which will only be trusted if they are strictly governed by the rule of law. It is in this general framework that the essential characteristics to be respected by an ASEAN Legal Service have to be designed.

In order to be useful, an ASEAN Legal Service will have to be trusted by all member states, and its advice must be sound, impartial and have a real authority. To reach these aims, one has to build a strong legal service, competent and independent, of the highest professional quality.

As the 2015 deadline is approaching quickly, one cannot start from a weak and modest legal service in the beginning, hoping that it will strengthen its knowledge, competence and authority through the years. Necessary conditions will have to be met from day one. There are two absolutely vital characteristics: first, independence; secondly, professional competence.

The interests of ASEAN as an organisation will not necessarily be congruent with those of the member states. Indeed, it may be in the interest of particular member states to keep ASEAN institutions weak. However, this would be fatal to the organisation in the long run. A neutral centre is vital if ASEAN is to progress, particularly in economic integration. The creation of a single market and investment area cannot occur if there is no neutral institution to oversee the implementation of the various treaty commitments. When it comes to giving of legal advice, the adviser must be independent of the member states. For effective settlement of disputes, the Legal Service cannot be biased. The Service must be impartial in order to be credible. The only way to create an ASEAN based on rule of law is to ensure the political neutrality of the central institutions. The independence of the Legal Service from the member states is thus absolutely vital.

The second essential characteristic is professional competence. This means that recruitment must be done on the basis of merit alone. There cannot be quotas for particular nationalities. Quotas based on nationality are a recipe for mediocrity or even downright incompetence. If one accepts the principle of independence, there is no justification for national quotas. The underlying rationale for such quotas is to secure national representation. The hidden subtext is that national representation is necessary to ensure the protection of national interests. The Legal Service cannot function on such a basis. The governing mantra must be 'the best person for the job', not 'jobs for the boys'.

3.4.3 Structure of the Legal Service

(3.4.3.1) Composition and hierarchy

The Legal Service should have a very senior member of the ASEAN Secretariat as its Head (viz., the Legal Counsel of ASEAN).

Two options may be envisaged. The first one would be to appoint a Director-General, as it has always been the case in the European Communities and in the EU. The second one, which would better take into account the political characteristics and specific political culture of ASEAN, would be to appoint a Deputy Secretary-General to be General Counsel.

The ASEAN Charter provides for four Deputy Secretaries-General with the rank and status of Deputy

3.4 STRUCTURE OF AN ASEAN LEGAL SERVICE

Ministers.[63] Of the four, two DSGs are to be openly recruited based on merit.[64] It is suggested that one of these two professionals should be appointed the Legal Counsel of ASEAN and Head of its Legal Service.

That will help to give an indisputable authority and a very senior rank to the Legal Counsel, as she/he will have to attend meetings at the highest level and will have the possibility of addressing them orally. The culture in ASEAN is hierarchical and status-conscious. A Legal Counsel with deputy-ministerial rank would carry some clout. It should be recalled that members of the Committee of Permanent Representatives (CPR) rank as ambassadors. The Head of the ASEAN Legal Service should be more senior to the members of the CPR if the post is to carry any authority. As it is, the interface between the CPR and the Secretary-General is unsettled. To appoint a Head of Legal Service with a status below that of the members of the CPR would invite micro-management of the Legal Service. This would compromise its neutrality.

A term of six years at least should be sufficient to allow her/him to develop her/his authority if she/he has the experience and authority needed. One of the problems of the current system is that there is no prospect of a long-term career once one reaches the rank of DSG. In 2012 ASEAN lost all four DSGs, despite the fact that at least one of the professionally recruited DSGs was willing to continue in office. The post of Legal Counsel of ASEAN is unlikely to attract candidates of acceptable quality if the appointment is only for three

---

[63] ASEAN Charter, Article 11(4).   [64] ASEAN Charter, Article 11(6)(b).

years. Three years would be too short to tempt a high-flying lawyer to give up her/his practice to serve in the ASEAN Legal Service. A guaranteed minimum of two three-year terms would be necessary for the recruitment of a competent candidate, subject of course to the possibility of non-renewal on the grounds of unsatisfactory performance or misbehaviour.

Under the authority of the DSG/Legal Counsel, it is suggested that three deputies should be appointed with the rank of Director. Their appointment should be based exclusively on merit. Each of the three should be responsible for one ASEAN Community Council. Therefore, one of them should probably be a 'lawyer/diplomat', the second one a 'lawyer/economist' and a third one might be a 'lawyer/academic'.

Each of the three Directors in the Legal Service should have a small team of competent and able lawyers to help them to serve as legal advisers of each of the Community Councils and of all sectoral ministerial bodies attached to them. The exact number of these lawyers will need to be worked out. It is not to be excluded that only some of them should be full-time officials. Given the complex legal work to be accomplished in an international community dealing with delicate matters, these lawyers should constitute an elite. While there will be a strong preference for ASEAN nationals to fill these positions, it might be necessary to admit a few non-ASEAN nationals as legal experts. A professional legal service needs the best people it can get; it may not be possible to find the necessary talent within ASEAN for some time to come. It should be made absolutely clear that it would not be possible to give any guarantee of an equal representation of ASEAN nationalities in the Legal

3.4 STRUCTURE OF AN ASEAN LEGAL SERVICE

Service. English-speaking lawyers of sufficient calibre are not common in every ASEAN country. Admission of candidates of unsatisfactory quality merely to satisfy a national quota would be a recipe for disaster. It would be fatal for the *esprit de corps* of the Legal Service if incompetent time-servers were recruited purely on the grounds of their nationality.

In addition to these full-time officers, and in order to enlarge the possibilities to strengthen the Legal Service, especially during the first years, one may envisage a list of consultants who would be able to work when needed, either part time or for ad hoc projects. The list should be drawn from law firms, and/or from universities or from former lawyers in an ASEAN member state or in another intergovernmental international organisation.

Despite this, it will be impossible to demand that a member of the Legal Service should participate at every one of all ASEAN meetings, as there are hundreds of these. Meetings of all bodies which are listed in Annex 1 of the Charter will therefore be attended only when necessary or useful, under instructions of the Legal Counsel. This means that the Legal Service will have to choose which meetings to attend in priority, i.e., most obviously meetings where legal issues are at stake, in particular when normative texts are being discussed. For other meetings, the member of the Legal Service specialising in the matter will be at the disposal of the Chair of the meeting, who might call that lawyer if and when needed.

In principle, only the Legal Counsel should attend the ASEAN Summit and the ASEAN Coordinating Council, while only the Directors in the Legal Service should participate in the Community Councils and in the Ministerial Meetings. The meetings of the Committee of Permanent Representatives (CPR) should be attended either by the Legal Counsel or by one of the three Directors. It seems that, up to now, the CPR has not played a central role. However, things might change in the future, with the multiplication of normative texts to be adopted. If one looks at the evolution of the equivalent body in the EU, viz., the 'COREPER' (Comité des représentants permanents/Committee of Permanent Representatives), its role has increased over the years. Many see it as the best technical body to prepare the European Council (the equivalent of the ASEAN Summits), playing an essential role in negotiating and drafting agreements and decisions. The Legal Counsel of the EU Council plays an important role in COREPER and attends any and each of its meetings, be it formal or informal (including lunches and dinners), and has the right to speak in the same way as any of the twenty-eight Ambassadors, the Permanent Representatives of the governments of the member states of the EU.[65]

(3.4.3.2) Recruitment

Recruitment should ensure that all members of the ASEAN Legal Service have the highest professional qualities and the fullest independence, with due regard to integrity,

---

[65] The Legal Counsel plays exactly the same role in all meetings of the Council of Ministers of the EU. He also attends all meetings of the European Council (which corresponds to the ASEAN Summit) and may intervene there, but only at the request of the President or other Members of the European Council.

3.4 STRUCTURE OF AN ASEAN LEGAL SERVICE

capability and professional experience and gender equality. In order to reach this goal, a panel should be constituted in order to check in an open competition the merits of the candidates: legal knowledge, capacity to work in an international environment in which several legal traditions are represented, capacity to give legal opinions in a concise and simple way, orally and in writing, and to give them with the utmost independence and impartiality.

The procedure should ensure a public appeal for candidates and an independent selection panel which could comprise judges or senior lawyers of any nationality. A candidate would have to send to the panel their detailed curriculum vitae, examples of their writings if any, and a letter of motivation. Those who are selected on a shortlist would be convened for an interview to test their capacities. Their ability to express a legal opinion and to defend it orally with brief, clear and decisive arguments should be particularly tested. In order to be a candidate to a post of Director in the Legal Service, experience of at least ten years as a lawyer should be required. As for the recruitment of the Legal Counsel themselves, the required length of experience should be at least fifteen years. The Legal Counsel, as a Deputy Secretary-General, shall be appointed by the ASEAN Summit, on the recommendation of the Secretary-General. In this respect the Secretary-General will have to be accorded real discretion, since the Legal Counsel would have to command the full confidence of the Secretary-General. This is unlikely to be the case if the Secretary-General is forced to accept a candidate selected by the CPR, for example.

(3.4.3.3) Salary and terms of service

Needless to say the level of salary must be competitive with the level of salary plus benefits of competent international lawyers. It will not be easy to attract candidates of sufficient calibre if salaries are pegged at an unrealistically low level. In Singapore, members of the Legal Service are paid on par with their contemporaries in private practice, at least for the first few years. It is not possible even in Singapore to match the salaries of partners of the top local and international legal firms. No international organisation funded by public money can realistically be expected to pay salaries of that level. However, that is not necessary as long as the members of the Legal Service feel that they are doing a satisfying job and are respected professionally.

The salary of the Legal Counsel should also take into account that a full career in the Legal Service will not be possible for her/him as, if the above suggestions were to be followed, the Legal Counsel, as an ASEAN DSG, would be subject to reappointment upon expiry of his term instead of having security of tenure until retirement. For example, in the EU, the basic annual salary of the Director General/Legal Counsel of the European Parliament, of the Council or of the Commission is approximately 200,000 to 220,000 euros,[66] or approximately US$265,000 to US$287,000 per annum. The ASEAN Legal Counsel may not require quite such a high salary, given the lower living costs in Jakarta (where she/he would presumably be based).

---

[66] See Article 66 of the EU Staff Regulations.

3.4 STRUCTURE OF AN ASEAN LEGAL SERVICE

(3.4.3.4) Legal status and guarantee of independence

It is of vital importance that the Legal Counsel and members of the Legal Service be insulated from political pressure from member states. The value of having an independent legal service is precisely that: it is independent of the member states and therefore can be counted on to act impartially. Moreover, deficiencies in pay and terms of service compared to the private sector can be compensated for if the members of the Legal Service feel that they are performing a valuable task, carrying with it professional satisfaction. This can only be fostered by ensuring that the Service is not buffeted by political winds.

Several articles of the ASEAN Charter aim at ensuring the independence of the members of the ASEAN Secretariat. Article 11(8)(b) provides that the staff of the Secretariat shall not seek or receive instructions from any government or external party outside ASEAN. Article 11(9) declares that 'each ASEAN member state undertakes to respect the exclusively ASEAN character of the responsibilities of the Secretary-General and the staff, and not to seek to influence them in the discharge of their responsibilities'. These commitments must be taken seriously if the Legal Service is to have any credibility.

On top of these legal guarantees conferred on the Secretariat, it is necessary that a reputation for impartiality for the Legal Service must be established. It would be useful to have an official declaration stressing that the Legal Service's opinions will always be free of any interference either by the Secretary-General or by the authorities of the member states, including the member state holding the ASEAN Chairmanship. It should also be made clear that Article 11(4) of the ASEAN Charter[67] does not put into question the independence of the Legal Counsel as to the content and orientation of the legal opinions given orally or in writing by the Legal Service. In the same way, it should be clarified that Article 7(2)(g) of the Charter, according to which the Secretary-General 'will serve with the confidence and at the pleasure of the Heads of State or Government', does not affect this basic principle of the independence of the Legal Service.

3.4.4 Mission Statement and Terms of Reference

Mission Statement

> To provide competent and unbiased legal advice to the ASEAN Summit, the Secretary-General and other ASEAN Organs in order to support the building of an ASEAN Community based on the rule of law.

Terms of Reference

1. The Legal Service is the legal advisor of ASEAN. It is placed under the direction of the ASEAN Legal Counsel, Deputy Secretary-General of ASEAN.
2. The Legal Service is administratively attached to the ASEAN Secretariat. Its opinions are given under the sole responsibility of the ASEAN Legal Counsel.

---

[67] ASEAN Charter, Article 11(4): 'The Deputy Secretaries-General shall be accountable to the Secretary-General in carrying out their functions.'

3.4 STRUCTURE OF AN ASEAN LEGAL SERVICE

3. The Legal Service shall assist ASEAN and all its organs, as enumerated in Chapter IV of the ASEAN Charter, in order to help to ensure the legality and quality of their acts, decisions and actions.
4. The Legal Service shall give consultative and independent opinions, orally or in writing, on any question of an institutional or legal nature.
5. The Legal Service may be requested to draft legal documents for the Secretariat and any other ASEAN organ. Any draft text submitted to an ASEAN organ and intended to have legal consequences shall be reviewed by the Legal Service and shall be accompanied by its written opinion.
6. The opinions of the Legal Service shall be internal to ASEAN. When presented in writing, they shall be sent to all ASEAN member states and to the interested ASEAN organs, under the responsibility of the ASEAN Legal Counsel.
7. The Legal Service shall be the legal memory of the ASEAN organs and of the ASEAN Secretariat. It is in charge of organising the archives and is the Depository of the international agreements concluded by the ASEAN.
8. The Legal Service shall be in charge of publishing all ASEAN texts having legal effect and shall keep a classified record of these texts and of their preparatory acts. It is in charge of the legal website of ASEAN.
9. The Legal Service may be requested to interpret the ASEAN Charter or any other ASEAN text, in accordance with the provisions of the Charter or any other ASEAN instrument.
10. The Legal Service shall provide legal support to the Secretary-General, the relevant sectoral ministers and

the ASEAN Secretariat in their task of monitoring the implementation of ASEAN's decisions.

11. The Legal Service shall provide all necessary legal support to the Secretary-General and various organs of ASEAN in the establishment of the three pillars of the ASEAN Community, namely the ASEAN Economic Community, the ASEAN Political-Security Community and the ASEAN Socio-Cultural Community.

12. The Legal Service may be tasked with legal support of any procedure, mechanism or organ, either ad hoc or permanent, which may be established within the framework of the ASEAN system for the settlement of disputes.

13. The Legal Service shall provide legal support to the ASEAN Summit upon reference to it of any unresolved dispute or non-compliance with the result of an ASEAN dispute settlement mechanism.

14. The Legal Service may represent, or instruct counsel to represent, ASEAN in any legal proceedings by or against ASEAN in any domestic or international forum.

EXECUTIVE SUMMARY

ASEAN was conceived in 1967 as a confidence-building measure to foster trust among the five original members of the association. The organisation has gradually expanded to cover all the states of Southeast Asia (with the exception of Timor Leste) and now extends to cooperation in practically all areas of the economy, foreign policy and government. This development, however, has been piecemeal and lacking in strategic impetus. An oft-ventilated criticism of ASEAN is that it is good at producing declarations, agreements, road maps and other instruments but bad at implementing them. The avowed goal of ASEAN is to create a community by 2015, comprising three pillars: the ASEAN Economic Community (AEC), the ASEAN Political-Security Community (APSC) and the ASEAN Socio-Cultural Community (ASCC). The primary framework document for this purpose is the ASEAN Charter. It is clearly stated in the Charter, and repeatedly re-emphasised subsequently, that the ASEAN Community will be rules-based and underpinned by the rule of law.

ASEAN has no ambition to become a supranational organisation with shared sovereignty. It will remain an organisation of nation states. For this reason, it is misleading to consider entities such as the EU as models. This is not what ASEAN aims to be, despite the reference in the Charter to an ASEAN Union. That may come in time, but not in the foreseeable future. The present goal, and one that will absorb the energy of the member states, will be the creation of the ASEAN Community. This cannot happen unless there is a culture of respecting the rules and following up on the many grand visions set out in various ASEAN instruments. Developing this 'rules-based' culture is vital to the creation of the ASEAN Community. Without that commitment to fulfilling the many obligations undertaken by the member states and following the rules they have agreed to, the ASEAN Community will be nothing but a mirage.

It is impossible to create a rules-based ASEAN Community without some means of drafting, interpreting and enforcing rules. The major shortcoming of ASEAN as an organisation is the inability to follow through on the many agreements, declarations, road maps and instruments that have proliferated over the years. The proliferation of such ASEAN documents creates a need for a centralised authority to ensure coherence and legal efficacy. An ASEAN Legal Service is necessary to ensure that the vital legal infrastructure of the ASEAN Community is properly developed. Without such a centralised service, the legal development of the ASEAN Community will continue to be ad hoc. There will be an increasing risk of incoherence, inconsistencies and even outright contradictions in the noodle-bowl of obligations entered into by ASEAN member states in the creation of the ASEAN Community. While it is possible to learn from the experiences of other intergovernmental organisations (both the bad as well as the good), any ASEAN Legal Service will have to be tailored to the Community, in the light of its history and culture. Therefore, there is no model that ASEAN can or should follow uncritically.

EXECUTIVE SUMMARY

Functions of the ASEAN Legal Service

An ASEAN Legal Service would have a significant role to play in the development of ASEAN as a rules-based, law-abiding organisation, in the following areas:

- drafting of agreements, rules and regulations for both internal as well as external purposes;
- providing the institutional legal memory of ASEAN by maintaining records, updating agreements and other legal instruments and ensuring that inconsistencies are resolved;
- providing impartial expert legal advice to the ASEAN Summit, the member states, the Secretary-General, the Community Councils, the ministerial bodies and the Committee of Permanent Representatives, as well as other ASEAN bodies;
- assisting the Secretary-General in monitoring the implementation of and compliance with ASEAN agreements;
- providing legal representation for ASEAN as an entity;
- assisting the ASEAN Summit, the Secretary-General and other dispute resolution bodies in the settlement of disputes.

(1) Drafting of agreements

ASEAN aims to be a rules-based organisation. Such an organisation needs clear rules. There are four aspects to this: first, the internal agreements that bind ASEAN member states and create the infrastructure of the organisation; secondly, the agreements between ASEAN and outside parties; thirdly, the internal rules and regulations necessary to realise the ASEAN single market and production base; and, fourthly, the

EXECUTIVE SUMMARY

harmonisation of the domestic laws of ASEAN member states. A rules-based organisation whose working language is English must have a core of competent legal draughtsmen. Apart from the issue of linguistic and legal competence, there is also the matter of political neutrality. An ASEAN Legal Service will be able to provide dedicated and continuous attention to the drafting of agreements. Experience in ASEAN affairs is essential for good drafting. This experience can only be accumulated if there is a proper legal service.

(2) **Institutional memory and avoidance of inconsistencies**

The ASEAN Summit, ASEAN Coordinating Committee, Community Councils, sectoral ministerial bodies and other organs of ASEAN will issue an increasing volume of documents as the ASEAN Community develops. The necessary expertise for drafting these documents and ensuring consistency and coherence can only be provided by a proper professional legal service that deals exclusively with ASEAN matters. The Legal Service should be responsible for monitoring the many agreements that emanate from the various meetings. The task of keeping track of these agreements and updating them as they are amended is also crucial. A rules-based organisation can only thrive if the rules can be found. There has to be an authoritative source for ASEAN agreements, rules and regulations.

(3) **Giving legal advice**

If ASEAN is to be taken seriously as a rules-based organisation, there must be an independent legal service uninfluenced

EXECUTIVE SUMMARY

by national agendas to render impartial legal advice to the ASEAN Summit and other organs of ASEAN. This is particularly the case where the ASEAN Economic Community is concerned, since economic integration requires the existence of a coherent and enforceable set of rules and regulations. Bodies like the AEM, the ASEAN Investment Area Council (AIA Council) and the Senior Economic Officials' Meeting (SEOM) are the key to the creation of a viable single market and production base. These bodies need to have access to impartial and credible legal advice in the discharge of their functions. The Secretary-General also requires strong legal backup to discharge the many tasks that he is entrusted with. The ASEAN Secretariat will also need legal advice in order to function efficiently, as does the Committee of Permanent Representatives. The legal services of the member states cannot fulfil the need for legal advice even if officers could be assigned on a long-term basis. There will always be the suspicion of national bias, whether conscious or unconscious. An independent ASEAN service is required if legal advice is to be credible and authoritative.

(4) Monitoring implementation of and compliance with ASEAN agreements

One major criticism of ASEAN is that implementation of agreements has not been consistent or effective. The Secretary-General is now entrusted with the function of monitoring compliance by member states with the obligations they have undertaken. He requires the assistance of legally trained officers in this task. This monitoring function

EXECUTIVE SUMMARY

is complementary to the task of maintaining the Table of Ratifications.

(5) Legal representation

ASEAN now has a legal personality separate from the member states. The intent of the Charter is to create a juridical person that can own property and enforce rights independently of the member states. Inevitably, ASEAN will become embroiled in legal disputes, whether involving commercial contracts, tenancies or employment matters. Representing ASEAN before legal tribunals would be a natural role for an ASEAN Legal Service.

(6) Settlement of disputes

The dispute settlement mechanisms established by the ASEAN Charter and other ASEAN instruments envisage a key role to be played by the ASEAN Summit, the Secretary-General, the Chairman of ASEAN and the ASEAN Coordinating Council. In discharging the vital function of ensuring the peaceful and legally binding settlement of disputes, especially in the economic sphere, it is essential that these organs be supported by competent and experienced legal officers. Only a proper legal service can develop the necessary experience and expertise in ASEAN dispute settlement. Crucially, only an ASEAN Legal Service can be counted on to be impartial and politically neutral in settling disputes amongst member states. An effective means of settling disputes is absolutely vital to the success of the ASEAN Community, particularly the ASEAN Economic Community.

EXECUTIVE SUMMARY

Structure of the Legal Service

The Legal Service should have a very senior member of the ASEAN Secretariat as its Head (viz., the Legal Counsel of ASEAN). The Legal Counsel of ASEAN should be openly recruited (i.e., not politically appointed by the member states) and have the rank of Deputy Secretary-General in order to ensure that she/he has sufficient status and seniority effectively to fulfil her/his crucial functions. The Legal Counsel should normally serve for two three-year terms; a shorter term of office will not allow the Legal Counsel adequate time to do the job, nor will it be attractive to candidates with the desired skills and experience.

There should be three deputies with the rank of Director. Their appointment should be based exclusively on merit and not to fill a national quota. Each should be responsible for one ASEAN Community Council, supported by a team of competent and able lawyers. Given the complex legal work to be accomplished in an international community dealing with delicate matters, these lawyers should constitute an elite. They should be openly recruited based on experience and competence.

While there will be a strong preference for ASEAN nationals to fill these positions, it might be necessary to admit a few non-ASEAN nationals as legal officers. A professional legal service needs the best people it can get; it may not be possible to find the necessary talent within ASEAN for some time to come. It should be made absolutely clear that it would not be possible to give any guarantee of an equal representation of ASEAN nationalities in the Legal Service. Admission of candidates of unsatisfactory quality merely to satisfy a national quota would be a recipe for disaster. It would be fatal for the *esprit de corps* of the Legal Service if incompetent persons were recruited purely on the grounds of their nationality.

In addition, there may be a list of consultants who would be able to work when needed, either part time or for ad hoc projects. The list should be drawn from law firms, and/or from universities or from former lawyers in an ASEAN member state or in another intergovernmental international organisation.

Recruitment should be by open application rather than nomination by member states. An independent panel comprising judges or senior lawyers of any nationality should be constituted to select suitable candidates. The level of salary and perks must be competitive with that of competent international lawyers. It will not be easy to attract candidates of sufficient calibre if salaries are pegged at an unrealistically low level.

It is of vital importance that the Legal Counsel and members of the Legal Service be insulated from political pressure from member states. The value of having an independent legal service is precisely that: it is independent of the member states and therefore can be counted on to act impartially. Moreover, deficiencies in pay and terms of service compared to the private sector can be compensated for if the members of the Legal Service feel that they are performing a valuable task, carrying with it professional satisfaction. This can only be fostered by ensuring that the Service is not buffeted by political winds.

Annex: major ASEAN agreements and declarations

Note: this list is not meant to be exhaustive.

Political and security

1967	Bangkok Declaration
1971	Zone of Peace, Freedom and Neutrality Declaration
1976	Declaration of ASEAN Concord (Bali Concord)
1976	Treaty of Amity and Cooperation in Southeast Asia
1976	Agreement on the Establishment of the ASEAN Secretariat
1995	Treaty on the Southeast Asia Nuclear Weapon-Free Zone
2003	Declaration of ASEAN Concord II (Bali Concord II)
2004	Treaty on Mutual Legal Assistance in Criminal Matters
2005	ASEAN Agreement on Disaster Management and Emergency Response
2007	ASEAN Convention on Counter-Terrorism
2007	ASEAN Charter
2009	Agreement on the Privileges and Immunities of ASEAN
2009	ASEAN Petroleum Security Agreement

ANNEX

2011 Declaration on ASEAN Community in a Global Community of Nations (Bali Concord III)
2012 ASEAN Human Rights Declaration

Economic

1979 Agreement on the ASEAN Food Security Reserve
1992 Agreement on the Common Effective Preferential Tariff (CEPT) Scheme for the ASEAN Free Trade Area
1992 Framework Agreement on Enhancing ASEAN Economic Cooperation
1995 ASEAN Framework Agreement on Services
1997 ASEAN Agreement on Customs
1998 ASEAN Framework Agreement on Mutual Recognition Arrangements
1998 Framework Agreement on the ASEAN Investment Area
1998 Framework Agreement on Facilitation of Goods in Transit
2000 e-ASEAN Framework Agreement
2002 Framework Agreement on Comprehensive Economic Cooperation between ASEAN and China
2003 Framework Agreement on Comprehensive Economic Cooperation between India and ASEAN
2003 Framework Agreement for Comprehensive Economic Partnership between Japan and ASEAN
2004 ASEAN Framework Agreement for Integration of Priority Sectors
2004 Protocol on Enhanced Dispute Settlement Mechanism

ANNEX

2005 Agreement to Establish and Implement the ASEAN Single Window
2005 Agreement on the Harmonized ASEAN Electrical and Electronic Equipment Regulatory Regime
2005 Framework Agreement on Comprehensive Economic Cooperation among the Governments of Member Countries of ASEAN and the Republic of Korea
2009 ASEAN Framework Agreement on the Facilitation of Inter-State Transport
2009 ASEAN Multilateral Agreement on Air Services
2009 ASEAN Multilateral Agreement on the Full Liberalisation of Air Freight Services
2009 ASEAN Trade in Goods Agreement
2009 ASEAN Comprehensive Investment Agreement
2009 Agreement Establishing the ASEAN-Australia-New Zealand Free Trade Area
2010 ASEAN Multilateral Agreement on Full Liberalisation of Passenger Air Services
2012 ASEAN Agreement on the Movement of Natural Persons

Socio-cultural

1985 ASEAN Agreement on Conservation of Nature and Natural Resources
2002 ASEAN Tourism Agreement
2002 ASEAN Agreement on Transboundary Haze Pollution

INDEX

AANZFTA (ASEAN-Australia-New Zealand Free Trade Area), 66
ACB (ASEAN Compliance Body), 44
ACC (ASEAN Coordinating Council), 56–7, 88–92, 111, 155, 175
ACMB (ASEAN Compliance Monitoring Body), 79
ACT (ASEAN Consultation to Solve Trade and Investment Issues), 44, 166
ADMM (ASEAN Defence Ministers' Meeting), 39
AEC (ASEAN Economic Community), xxiii, xxvii, 44, 78, 108
AECC (ASEAN Economic Community Council), 52–7, 156
AEM (ASEAN Economic Ministers' Meeting), 19, 24–8, 80, 159
AFMM (ASEAN Finance Ministers' Meeting), 38
African Union, legal service observations from, 133, 135–6
AFTA (ASEAN Free Trade Area) and AFTA Council, 20, 26–7, 31, 35, 82

AHMM (ASEAN Ministers of Health), 37
AHRD (ASEAN Human Rights Declaration), 55, 112, 167
AIA (ASEAN Investment Area) and AIA Council, 26–8, 159
AICHR (ASEAN Intergovernmental Commission on Human Rights), 69, 167
AIPO (ASEAN Inter-Parliamentary Organisation), 47
ALAWMM (ASEAN Law Ministers' Meeting), 37
ALMM (ASEAN Labour Ministers), 36
AMAF (ASEAN Ministers of Agriculture and Forestry), 36
AMCA (ASEAN Ministers Responsible for Culture and the Arts), 39
AMM (ASEAN Ministerial Meeting), 16–40, 176
AMME (ASEAN Ministerial Meeting on the Environment), 37
AMMin (ASEAN Ministerial Meeting on Minerals), 39

INDEX

AMMST (ASEAN Ministerial Meeting on Science and Technology), 37
AMMTC (ASEAN Ministerial Meeting on Transnational Crime), 38
AMRI (ASEAN Ministers Responsible for Information), 37
Amsterdam, Treaty of (1996), 130
Andean Community, legal service observations from, 133, 135–6
Andean Pact, 133
Angkor Wat, ownership of, 86, 94
APSC (ASEAN Political-Security Community), xxiii, xxvii, 43, 45, 108–9, 111
APSC (ASEAN Political-Security Community Council), 52–7, 156
arbitration, 75, 78, 88–90
ASC (ASEAN Standing Committee), 16–17, 40
ASCC (ASEAN Socio-Cultural Community), xxiii, xxvii, 43, 45, 108, 110–11
ASCC (ASEAN Socio-Cultural Community Council), 52–7, 156
ASEAN. See Association of Southeast Asian Nations
ASEAN Agreement on Transboundary Haze Pollution (2002), 51
ASEAN Chambers of Commerce and Industry (ASEANCCI), 47

ASEAN Charter, xxvi, 40–9
ASEC and, 57–61
Bali Concord II paving way for, 23
Community Councils and, 52–7
CPR and, 61–4
drafting process, 67–70
DSM in, 49–52, 71–2
functions of ASEAN legal service and, 145–7
idealism as primary driver of, xxiii
interpretation of, 158
Kuala Lumpur Declaration on Establishment of, 40
separate ASEAN legal service and, 148
ASEAN Chiefs of National Police (ASEANAPOL), 38
ASEAN Community, building, 108–12, 184
AEC, xxiii, xxvii, 44, 78, 108
AHRD and, 111
APSC, xxiii, xxvii, 43, 45, 108–9, 111
ASCC, xxiii, xxvii, 43, 45, 108, 110–11
Bali II and, 108, 112
Bali III and, 111
blueprints for, 108–10, 152–3
legal basis required for, 108, 110, 112
ASEAN Community Councils. See Community Councils
ASEAN Compliance Body (ACB), 44

INDEX

ASEAN Compliance Monitoring Body (ACMB), 79
ASEAN Consultation to Solve Trade and Investment Issues (ACT), 44, 166
ASEAN Coordinating Council (ACC), 56-7, 88-92, 111, 155, 175
ASEAN Defence Ministers' Meeting (ADMM), 39
ASEAN Economic Community (AEC), xxiii, xxvii, 44, 78, 108
ASEAN Economic Community Council (AECC), 52-7, 156
ASEAN Economic Ministers' Meeting (AEM), 19, 24-8, 80, 159
ASEAN Education Ministers (ASED), 36
ASEAN Finance Ministers' Meeting (AFMM), 38
ASEAN Free Trade Area (AFTA) and AFTA Council, 20, 26-7, 31, 35, 82
ASEAN Human Rights Declaration (AHRD), 55, 112, 167
ASEAN Institutes of Strategic and International Studies (ASEAN-ISIS), 47
ASEAN Inter-Parliamentary Organisation (AIPO), 47
ASEAN Intergovernmental Commission on Human Rights (AICHR), 69, 167
ASEAN Investment Area (AIA) and AIA Council, 26-8, 159

ASEAN-ISIS (ASEAN Institutes of Strategic and International Studies), 47
ASEAN Labour Ministers (ALMM), 36
ASEAN Law Ministers' Meeting (ALAWMM), 37
ASEAN Legal Service, xxvii, 182, 184-90. *See also* functions of a legal service
composition and hierarchy, 172-6
decision-making process, 140-4
dispute settlement and, 144, 163-7
essential characteristics of, 170-2
EU system, observations from, 113-32
impartiality, importance of, 149, 171
implementation and monitoring of legal obligations, 137, 144, 160-2
international organisations generally, observations from, 132-45
legal status of, 179-80
mission statement for, 180
nationality of staff and member state representation, 174
necessity for, 147-51
professional competence, importance of, 172, 176-7
recruitment of staff, 176-7
salary and terms of service for staff, 178

INDEX

single, separate, independent service, necessity for, 147–51, 168, 171, 179–80
sizes of member states and decision-making process, 141
structure of, 167, 189–90
terms of reference for, 180–2
trust, importance of, 167, 171
ASEAN Ministerial Meeting (AMM), 16–40, 176
ASEAN Ministerial Meeting on Minerals (AMMin), 39
ASEAN Ministerial Meeting on Science and Technology (AMMST), 37
ASEAN Ministerial Meeting on the Environment (AMME), 37
ASEAN Ministerial Meeting on Transnational Crime (AMMTC), 38
ASEAN Ministers of Agriculture and Forestry (AMAF), 36
ASEAN Ministers of Health (AHMM), 37
ASEAN Ministers Responsible for Culture and the Arts (AMCA), 39
ASEAN Ministers Responsible for Information (AMRI), 37
ASEAN Political-Security Community (APSC), xxiii, xxvii, 43, 45, 108–9, 111
ASEAN Political-Security Community Council (APSC), 52–7, 156

ASEAN Secretary-General and Secretariat (ASEC). *See* Secretary-General and Secretariat
ASEAN Senior Law Officials' Meeting (ASLOM), 37, 70
ASEAN Senior Officials' Meeting (ASEAN SOM), 17
ASEAN Senior Officials on Drug Matters (ASOD), 38
ASEAN Socio-Cultural Community (ASCC), xxiii, xxvii, 43, 45, 108, 110–11
ASEAN Socio-Cultural Community Council (ASCC), 52–7, 156
ASEAN SOM (ASEAN Senior Officials' Meeting), 17
ASEAN Standing Committee (ASC), 16–17, 40
ASEAN Summit, 18–24, 81, 92, 155, 165, 175–6
ASEAN Telecommunications and IT Ministers' Meeting (TELMIN), 39
ASEAN Tourism Ministers' Meeting (M-ATM), 38
ASEAN Transport Ministers' Meeting (ATM), 38
ASEAN Union, as ultimate aim, 48, 65, 150, 183
ASEAN–Australia–New Zealand Free Trade Area (AANZFTA), 66
ASEAN+3, 23
ASEANAPOL (ASEAN Chiefs of National Police), 38

INDEX

ASEANCCI (ASEAN Chambers of Commerce and Industry), 47
ASEC. *See* Secretary-General and Secretariat
ASED (ASEAN Education Ministers), 36
Asian economic crisis (1997–8), 41
ASLOM (ASEAN Senior Law Officials' Meeting), 37, 70
ASOD (ASEAN Senior Officials on Drug Matters), 38
Association of Southeast Asian Nations (ASEAN), 183–90. *See also entries at* ASEAN
    DSM in (*See* dispute settlement mechanism)
    English as working language of, 69–71
    EU, not completely comparable to, 145
    historical development of, xxv, 1–16, 183
    institutional framework, 16–40
    major agreements and declarations, 191–3
    making rules in, 66–71
    rule-based community, importance of establishing, xxiii, 108, 110, 112, 184. (*See also* ASEAN Legal Service)
    suspicion and distrust within, 14–16
ATM (ASEAN Transport Ministers' Meeting), 38
Australia
    as dialogue partner, 23
    intergovernmental agreements with ASEAN, 66

Bali Concord I (1976), 11, 19, 24, 72
Bali Concord II (2003), 22, 27, 43–4, 108, 112
Bali Concord III (2011), xxiii, 55, 111, 147–8
Bangkok Declaration (1967), 6, 71
Brunei
    English proficiency in, 70
    formation and membership in ASEAN, 7

Cambodia
    accession to ASEAN, 14, 93
    Angkor Wat, ownership of, 86, 94
    English proficiency in, 70
    on South China Sea issue, 15
    Preah Vihear temple dispute, 77, 83, 86, 93–107, 164
    Vietnamese invasion of, 12–13, 15, 19
Cebu Declaration on the Blueprint for the ASEAN Charter, 47
CEPT (Common Effective Preferential Tariff) Scheme, 20, 26, 31, 35
Chair of ASEAN, 86, 106
China
    framework agreement with, 23
    in ASEAN+3, 23
    intergovernmental agreements with ASEAN, 66
    South China Sea issue and, 15

INDEX

chronologies
  of ASEAN development, 1–6
  of EU history, 113
  of major ASEAN agreements and declarations, 191–3
CLMV countries, 14–15, 44, 70. *See also* Cambodia; Laos; Myanmar; Vietnam
Colombia, ICJ ruling in territorial delimitation case against, 104
Committee of Permanent Representatives (CPR), 61–4, 173, 176
common agreement or common accord, decision-making by, 142
Common Effective Preferential Tariff (CEPT) Scheme, 20, 26, 31, 35
Community Councils, 52–7
  AECC, 52–7, 156
  APSC, 52–7, 156
  ASCC, 52–7, 156
  ASEAN Legal Service and, 156, 169, 176
  CPR and, 63
compliance with, implementation, and monitoring of legal obligations, 137, 144, 160–2, 187
consensus, decision-making by, 142
Council of Europe, legal service observations from, 133–7, 142–4
CPR (Committee of Permanent Representatives), 61–4, 173, 176

decision-making process, 140–4
Declaration on the Roadmap for the ASEAN Community (2009–15), 57, 152, 167
Deputy Secretaries-General (DSGs), 33, 60, 172
Dharsono, Hartono Rekso, 29
dispute settlement mechanism (DSM), 71–107
  adjudication provisions, 75, 87
  Angkor Wat, ownership of, 86, 94
  arbitration provisions, 75, 78, 88–90
  ASEAN Charter and, 49–52, 71–2
  ASEAN Legal Service and, 144, 163–7, 188
  ASEAN Summit, role of, 165
  Bali Concord II on, 44
  Chair of ASEAN and, 86, 106
  DSM Protocol (Protocol to the ASEAN Charter on Dispute Settlement Mechanisms), 72, 78, 84–91, 105
  economic disputes, 84
  EPG recommendations on, 49–52, 86, 164
  Manila Protocol, 78
  non-compliance with, 91–2
  non-economic disputes, 84–91
  of WTO, 81–4
  Pedra Branca dispute between Malaysia and Singapore, 102
  political nature of decision to submit to, 100–4
  Preah Vihear temple dispute, 77, 83, 86, 93–107, 164

199

INDEX

dispute settlement mechanism (DSM), (cont.)
 Secretary-General and, 85, 107
 Sipadan and Ligitan, dispute between Indonesia and Malaysia over, 76, 78, 102
 TAC, 50, 72–8, 85, 91, 102, 106–7
 territorial disputes, weakness of adjudication process regarding, 104
 Vientiane Protocol, 50–1, 72, 84–5, 89, 107, 164
 ZOPFAN on, 71
drafting agreements, as function of ASEAN Legal Service, 152–5, 185
DSGs (Deputy Secretaries-General), 33, 60, 172
DSM. *See* dispute settlement mechanism

economic disputes, 84
Eminent Persons' Group (EPG), xxiii, 46–9
 Community Councils and, 52–7
 DSM recommendations, 49–52, 86, 164
 on ASEAN Union, as ultimate aim, 48, 65, 150
 on ASEC, 57–61
 on CPR, 61–4
 on implementation and monitoring of legal obligations, 160
English, as working language of ASEAN, 69–71, 154

EPG. *See* Eminent Persons' Group
Europe, legal service observations from Council of, 133–7, 142–4
European Economic Area, 72–8
European Free Trade Area, 72–8
European Parliament, 127, 132, 141, 143, 168
European Union
 answering questions and handling informal complaints in, 138
 as dialogue partner, 23
 ASEAN not completely comparable to, 145
 chronology for, 113
 Commission, legal services of, 122–6, 137, 141, 168
 COREPER, 176
 Council, legal services of, 127–32, 141–4, 168, 176
 Draft Constitution for Europe (2003), 130
 infringement procedure in, 116–18
 interpretation of law in, 136
 legal order for, 113–16
 legal services in institutions of, 113–32, 135, 140
 legislative quality in, 131
 Official Journal, publication of acts in, 134
 preliminary ruling procedure in, 119–21
 sizes of member states and decision-making process, 141

INDEX

Framework Agreement for Integration of Priority Sectors (2004), 35, 45
Framework Agreement on Enhancing ASEAN Economic Cooperation (1992), 20, 26, 34, 78
Framework Agreement on Goods in Transit (1998), 35
functions of a legal service, 145–67, 185–8
  answering questions and handling informal complaints, 137–8
  as institutional memory, 133–4, 155–7, 186
  as legal interpreter of normative texts, 136, 158
  as legal representative before judicial organs, 139–40, 162–3, 188
  ASEAN Charter, fulfilling, 145–7
  dispute settlement, 144, 163–7, 188
  drafting agreements, 152–5, 185
  formal complaints, assistance in dealing with, 138–9
  implementation of, compliance with, and monitoring of legal obligations, 137, 144, 160–2, 187
  international organisations, observations on legal services of, 133–40, 151
  legal advice, providing, 135–6, 157–60, 186–7
  legal assistance to organisational bodies, providing, 137

  necessity for separate legal service and, 147–51

General Agreement on Trade in Services (GATS), 26

Hanoi Action Plan, 41, 45
historical development of ASEAN, xxv, 1–16, 183
Hor Namhong, 85, 87, 97–8
Hun Sen, 14, 93, 101

ICJ (International Court of Justice), 76, 78, 95, 99, 102, 104–5
IMF (International Monetary Fund), legal service observations from, 133, 135, 137, 140
implementation of, compliance with, and monitoring of legal obligations, 137, 144, 160–2, 187
India
  as dialogue partner, 23
  intergovernmental agreements with ASEAN, 66
Indonesia
  English proficiency in, 70
  formation of Malaysia, opposition to, 7
  in Vietnam War, 10
  MacDonald House bombing, 8–10
  Sipadan and Ligitan, dispute with Malaysia over, 76, 78, 102

201

INDEX

infringement procedure in EU, 116–18
institutional memory, legal services functioning as, 133–4, 155–7, 186
International Court of Justice (ICJ), 76, 78, 95, 99, 102, 104–5
International Monetary Fund (IMF), legal service observations from, 133, 135, 137, 140
interpretation
 as function of a legal service, 136, 158
 of ASEAN Charter, 158
 of EU law, 136

Japan
 in ASEAN+3, 23
 intergovernmental agreements with ASEAN, 66
 Takeshima/Dokdo dispute with South Korea, 104
 Joint Ministerial Meeting (JMM), 22–3, 25

Kasit Piromya, 97–8
Konfrontasi, 8
Korea, Republic of
 in ASEAN+3, 23
 intergovernmental agreements with ASEAN, 66
 Takeshima/Dokdo dispute with Japan, 104
Kuala Lumpur Declaration on Establishment of ASEAN Charter, 40

languages
 English, as working language of ASEAN, 69–71, 154
 used by legal services of international organisations, 134
Laos
 accession to ASEAN, 13
 English proficiency in, 70
legal services. *See* ASEAN Legal Service; functions of a legal service
Ligitan and Sipadan, dispute between Indonesia and Malaysia over, 76, 78, 102
Lisbon, Treaty of (2000), 130, 143

M-ATM (ASEAN Tourism Ministers' Meeting), 38
Maastricht, Treaty of (1991), 130
MacDonald House bombing, 8–10
making rules in ASEAN, 66–71
Malaysia
 English proficiency in, 70
 formation of, 7–9
 in Vietnam War, 10
 Pedra Branca dispute with Singapore, 102
 Sabah, dispute with Philippines over, 71
 Sipadan and Ligitan, dispute with Indonesia over, 76, 78, 102
Manila Protocol on Dispute Settlement Mechanism, 78
mission statement for ASEAN Legal Service, 180

202

INDEX

monitoring of, implementation of, and compliance with legal obligations, 137, 144, 160-2, 187
Myanmar
  accession to ASEAN, 13
  English proficiency in, 70

Natalegawa, Marty, 97-8, 106, 164
New Zealand and ASEAN, intergovernmental agreements between, 66
Nice, Treaty of (2000), 130
Norodom Ranariddh, Prince, 14, 93
Norodom Sihanouk, Prince, 95
North American Free Trade Area, 136

Ong Keng Yong, 68, 86, 148
Organisation for Economic Co-operation and Development (OECD), 134
Organization of American States (OAS), legal service observations from, 133, 135-6

Panyarachun, Anand, 61
Pedra Branca dispute between Malaysia and Singapore, 102
Pham Gia Khiem, 87, 97
Philippines
  English proficiency in, 69
  formation of Malaysia, opposition to, 8
  in Vietnam War, 9
  on South China Sea issue, 15
  Sabah, dispute with Malaysia over, 71
  WTO dispute with Thailand, 82-3
Post-Ministerial Conferences (PMCs), 18
Preah Vihear temple dispute, 77, 83, 86, 93-107, 164
preliminary ruling procedure in EU, 119-21

qualified majority voting (QMV), 142

Ramos, Fidel, 150
Roadmap for the ASEAN Community (2009-15), Declaration on, 57, 152, 167
Romulo, Carlos, 40, 150
Roxas, Mar, 82
rule-based community, importance of establishing ASEAN as, xxiii, 108, 110, 112, 184
rule-making in ASEAN, 66-71
rules for decision-making process, 140-4

Sabah, Malaysia-Philippines dispute over, 71
SEANFZ (Southeast Asia Nuclear Weapon-Free Zone), 21
Secretary-General and Secretariat (ASEC), 57-61
  ASEAN Legal Service and, 148, 159-67, 170
  CPR and, 63
  DSM and, 85, 107

203

INDEX

Secretary-General and Secretariat (ASEC), (cont.)
  history of ASEAN and, 29–36
Senior Economic Officials' Meeting (SEOM), 21, 24–8, 35, 78, 80–1, 159
settlement of disputes. *See* dispute settlement mechanism
simple majority voting, 143
Singapore
  ejection from Malaysian federation, 8
  English proficiency in, 69
  in Vietnam War, 10
  MacDonald House bombing, 8–10
  Pedra Branca dispute with Malaysia, 102
Singapore Declaration (1992), 20
Sipadan and Ligitan, dispute between Indonesia and Malaysia over, 76, 78, 102
sizes of member states and decision-making process, 141
South China Sea issue, 15
South Korea. *See* Korea, Republic of
Southeast Asia Nuclear Weapon-Free Zone (SEANFZ), 21
Surin Pitsuwan, 107

TAC (Treaty of Amity and Cooperation), 11, 19, 50, 72–8, 85, 91, 102, 106–7
TELMIN (ASEAN Telecommunications and IT Ministers' Meeting), 39

territorial disputes, weakness of adjudication process regarding, 104
Thailand
  Angkor Wat, ownership of, 86, 94
  English proficiency in, 70
  in Vietnam War, 9
  Preah Vihear temple dispute, 77, 83, 86, 93–107, 164,
  WTO dispute with Philippines, 82–3
Thaksin Shinawatra, 96, 101
Transit Transport Coordinating Board, 35
Treaty of Amity and Cooperation (TAC), 11, 19, 50, 72–8, 85, 91, 102, 106–7

UN Charter, 76
UN General Assembly
  decision-making process in, 140
  TAC endorsed by, 19
UN legal service observations, 133–6, 140
UN Security Council (UNSC) and Preah Vihear temple dispute, 98
unanimity, decision-making by, 142
United States, as ASEAN dialogue partner, 23

Vientiane Action Programme (VAP), 45, 57
Vientiane Protocol on the Enhanced Dispute

204

INDEX

Settlement Mechanism, 50–1, 72, 84–5, 89, 107, 164
Vietnam
  accession to ASEAN, 13
  Cambodia, invasion of, 12–13, 15, 19
  English proficiency in, 70
  on South China Sea issue, 15
Vietnam War, 9–12, 18
Vision 2020, 41

Wong Kan Seng, 15

Working Group for an ASEAN Human Rights Mechanism, 47
World Trade Organization (WTO).
  DSM, 81–4
  legal service observations from, 133, 135–7
  Textile Monitoring Body, 79

Yeo, George, 82, 86, 96, 99, 106

ZOPFAN Declaration (1971), 11, 71

For EU product safety concerns, contact us at Calle de José Abascal, 56–1°,
28003 Madrid, Spain or eugpsr@cambridge.org.

www.ingramcontent.com/pod-product-compliance
Ingram Content Group UK Ltd.
Pitfield, Milton Keynes, MK11 3LW, UK
UKHW050223060825
461487UK00023B/1767